Bringin' 'Em Back ALIVE

Reaching Your World for Jesus

Danny Lehmann

BRINGIN' 'EM BACK ALIVE

Danny Lehmann

Copyright © 1987 by Danny Lehmann
Printed in the United States of America
ISBN: 0-88368-199-4

Edited and designed by David L. Young.

Cover design by Cindy Feustal.

Unless otherwise noted, Bible quotations are taken from the *New American Standard Bible*, copyright © The Lockman Foundation, 1960, 1962, 1963, 1968, 1971, 1972, 1973, 1975, 1977 and used by permission.

DEDICATION

On July 9, 1982, gospel singer Keith Green and Loren Cunningham, President of *Youth With A Mission,* met together to pray for world missions. Aware of the tremendous need for workers, they agreed to believe the Lord of the Harvest for the release of 100,000 North American young people to the mission field. Three weeks later Keith was killed in a tragic plane crash, but the prayer he and Loren had prayed was recorded in heaven (Revelation 5:8). This book is dedicated to seeing their prayer answered—even exceeded.

Now to Him who is able to do exceeding abundantly beyond all that we ask or think, according to the power that works within us, to Him be the glory in the church and in Christ Jesus to all generations forever and ever. Amen—Ephesians 3:20-21.

ACKNOWLEDGEMENTS

Thanks to:

Linda, Daniel, and David for their love and encouragement;

Kevin White and Jeff Brow for leading me to Jesus;

Kalafi Moala, Loren Cunningham, Francis Anfuso, and Arthur Blessitt for their example and vision;

Pastors Garry Ansdell, Mark Buckley, Johnny Johnston, Mike Kiley, Frank O'Neill, Bill Stonebraker, and Chuck Smith for much needed counsel and teaching;

Geoff Benge for his labor of love in editing this second edition;

and Jennie Ogden for typing the manuscript.

CONTENTS

Foreword By

Loren Cunningham

Paul said to the Romans, "I commend to you our sister Phoebe, who is a servant of the church which is at Cenchrea; that you receive her in the Lord in a manner worthy of the saints" (Romans 16:1-2). And in Second Corinthians 8:16 Paul introduces Titus, showing his task, calling, character, and relationship to himself and the church.

It is *my* privilege to introduce to you a fellow worker of mine and yours in Christ, Danny Lehmann. Since his conversion on the beaches of California, Danny has never looked back. Not only has Danny grown in the grace and knowledge of our Lord Jesus, but he has taken his place in the Body of Christ in leadership and as an Evangelist with a capital "E." Wherever he goes in North America, Asia, or the South Pacific, Danny bears "fruit that remains." He has not only the experience but the spiritual authority to write on soul-winning. Danny doesn't just take opportunities to share Christ—he *makes* them.

Bringin' 'Em Back Alive is a fast reading, hard-hitting book that will not only hold your interest but will challenge you, instruct you, inspire you, and guide you to make your life count in leading others to Christ and eternal life. You're in for an adventure.

Loren Cunningham
President, *Youth With a Mission*

Foreword By
Chuck Smith

It has been my privilege to know Danny Lehmann for several years and have the opportunity to watch him develop in his spiritual walk and growth. I know of no one who can speak with greater authority on the subject of modern day missions—the need, and how to meet the need of reaching our world to share with them the love of Jesus Christ.

Danny does not speak from theory developed in a classroom or methods hatched in a conference room. He speaks from the practical experience of being in the trenches *doing it*. When Danny speaks on missions, which is the passion of his heart, I listen and learn.

Chuck Smith
Pastor, *Calvary Chapel,* Costa Mesa

Introduction

Someone once said that compared to evangelism everything else happening in the church is like rearranging the furniture while the house is on fire. Such a statement may seem radical and extreme to some, but it should help us see the urgency of the task our Lord has laid before us. From the jungles of Papua New Guinea to the streets of Amsterdam and Beverly Hills, there are men and women who are eternally lost, living in spiritual darkness and alienated from God. As we proceed in this book, we will see that Scripture plainly teaches they will stay that way unless someone cares for them enough to go and lead them from their lost state to the Light.

One of the most tragic phrases uttered in the Bible is found in Psalm 142:4, where the Psalmist declares, "No man cared for my soul" (*KJV*). This question should be on the lips of every potential soul-winner: *Do I Care?* Do I care about and love those who are dying every day without Christ?

If you do care, or if you want to start caring, then I trust this book will help you develop a caring *lifestyle* of evangelism. Success in evangelism depends not so much on talent and ability but on whether or not we truly care. Both Jesus and Paul told us that love should be the bottom

11

line of everything we do in the Christian life, and this is nowhere more true than when it comes to evangelism.

This book is written out of a sense of urgency and hope. Urgency—because despite the headway the gospel is making around the world, the church continues to grow at a slower pace than the population. Urgency—because while sin continues unchecked in our world, it causes incredible pain and suffering. But, most of all, urgency—because God's heart breaks every time another soul slips into a Christless eternity.

Bringin' 'Em Back Alive is written also in the hope that the people of God will take the Great Commission seriously, mobilize, and see the task completed. It is the hope that springs from faith in a God who wants the job done and that the kingdoms of this world will eventually become the kingdoms of our Lord and of His Christ. (See Revelation 11:15.)

This book is written with one purpose in mind—that of recruiting and equipping volunteers for God's army who will, in turn, commit themselves to finishing the task Jesus Christ has given us. (See John 4:34.) *Bringin' 'Em Back Alive* is geared for both the Christian in the nine-to-five workaday world and the prospective missionary candidate. While not all of us are called to be cross-cultural evangelists, we are all called to be *witnesses*. This book will examine the motives, message, and methods a witness must have and use. We will examine them in the light of God's Word, our final authority.

A Lifestyle Of Evangelism

The apostle Paul didn't see evangelism as the job of slick professionals but as the work of every Christian called of

God. (See Ephesians 4:11-13.) He didn't have a department store mentality when it came to evangelism. In his life, evangelism wasn't stuffed into a corner, like the shoe department at Sears, or occasionally visited when it was "outreach time."

Paul tells us that he did *all things* for the sake of the gospel. (See 1 Corinthians 9:20-23.) He had developed a "lifestyle" of evangelism, and his whole life was committed to spreading the good news. Whether preaching on Mars Hill, discipling Timothy, planting churches, or making tents, Paul's life was consumed with his relationship to Jesus and the task the Lord had given him: "To preach to the Gentiles the unfathomable riches of Christ" (Ephesians 3:8).

There is a temptation to relegate this type of lifestyle to spiritual giants, or super-Christians, like Paul: "Yeah, well that's fine for him; he was an apostle. I'm not."

Paul knew he would be put on a pedestal, so he took pains to show that he was just the same as every other Christian, even going so far as to call himself the "chief of sinners" (1 Timothy 1:15). While he made it clear not all are called to be apostles, he exhorted us to imitate his lifestyle. (See 1 Corinthians 11:1; 12:1-31; Philippians 3:17; 4:9.) The main thrust of Paul's teaching was that all Christians are called to be functioning parts of the Body, working together to see that it multiplies and grows. (See Ephesians 4:16.)

Romans 10:14 makes the nature of evangelism quite clear. Paul tells us that people can't be saved unless they hear the word, so we must preach it! For many of us such a command is frightening. It need not be. There are three Greek words used in the New Testament in relation to spreading the gospel, but only one of them, *kerusso*—to "proclaim like a herald"—concerns street corner type preaching. The other two—*euggeizoai*, to "tell good news," and *martureo*, to "bear witness"—simply mean to share the gospel and bear witness to the truth by whatever means we can.

Michael Green, noted Anglican author, said, "When men have the will to speak of their Lord they find no shortage of ways to do it."[1] Many of us don't feel called to street corner preaching, but, as we seek the Lord, He will show us numerous ways we can share His love with the lost.

Some recent surveys have revealed that up to 90 percent of Christians in the church today have never led a soul to Christ. On the other hand, the American Institute of Church Growth reports that 86 percent of believers active in the church today are there because of a personal contact they had with a concerned Christian.[2]

Imagine the phenomenal growth there would be in churches if *every* Christian, not just 10 percent, were having personal contact with unbelievers and leading them to Jesus!

I believe one of the major items on God's agenda right now is a revival in the area of personal evangelism. There needs to be a renewed emphasis, both from the pulpit and in the pew, on the responsibility God has placed on all of us to win souls. The church needs evangelists who will take the time to equip the saints in evangelism and pastors who will encourage their congregations to get involved in the task. We need to see godly leaders, both men and women, demonstrate a lifestyle of evangelism and sound the trumpet of war as they lead us onto the front lines of evangelism.

We need, however, to be vaccinated against a disease I call "Areopagitus," which had infected the philosophers on Mars Hill. (See Acts 17:19-21.) The main symptom of this disease is a fascination with anything "new." While the tear-filled eyes of a broken-hearted heavenly Father scan the earth for laborers to work in His harvest field, we are busy giving our energy to the latest new sensation that is taking the church by storm, be it Christian diets, dating, self-esteem, mood-control, exercise programs, or the latest "new" revelation from one of the watchdogs of God's flock. Oh, for a return to the simple, Beelzebub-bustin', devil-stompin', holy boldness and fiery zeal that sent the "normal" everyday disciples in the early church "everywhere preaching the Word" (Acts 8:4, *KJV*).

1

Needed—A Volunteer Army

CHAPTER ONE

Needed—A Volunteer Army

"Thy people will volunteer freely in the day of Thy power; in holy array, from the womb of the dawn, Thy youth are to Thee as the dew"—Psalm 110:3.

We live at an exciting point in human history! The prophet Joel and the apostle Peter both spoke of an army that God would raise up in that period known as the *last days*, upon whom He would pour out His Spirit. This army would use the dreams of the old and the vision and energy of the young to prophesy, or speak forth God's anointed word, to their generation. To His children of the last days, He promises not only the anointing that comes from being Spirit-filled but also that they will receive a special anointing to proclaim the gospel in the end-times. (See Acts 2:17-21.)

While they might not agree on all the particulars, most Bible scholars today believe we are living in the last days. Throughout the worldwide Body of Christ is the cry that God is preparing His people for a great thrust of evangelism destined to reach every corner of the earth and usher multitudes into the Kingdom of God.

Just as in any army, success in battle depends on the obedience of each individual soldier to the orders of the commander-in-chief. So, too, in God's end-time army we must be willing and ready to obey those orders that come down to us from our Commander-in-Chief. Indeed, He has already issued His command—GO!

The need for world evangelism has never been greater, but neither has the potential to meet that need been as great as it is today. In 1974, the church reeled as Ralph Winter, speaking at the Lausanne Congress on World Evangelism, laid out the magnitude of the task of world evangelism still to be done. We learned that there were 16,750 distinct people groups that accounted for nearly three billion people who were either culturally, linguistically, socially, or geographically removed from any existing church or mission. Moreover, many of these groups are resistant to the gospel and located in countries where it is nearly impossible to go as a tourist, let alone obtain a missionary visa.

Such facts and figures can make us depressed and apathetic about the whole thing, but we need to stop being impressed by Satan's dominion in the earth and start crying out to God for His Kingdom to come and His will to be done on earth as it is in heaven. Rather than concerning ourselves with doors that are closed to the gospel, we must make sure we take advantage of all the open doors before it is too late.

Samuel Zwemer, a pioneer missionary to the Muslim world, said, "Opportunism is not the last word in missions. The open door beckons; the closed door challenges him who has a right to enter."

God Of The Impossible

When we begin to think seriously about world evangelism, it seems an impossible task. To establish a church in every one of the 16,750 people groups by the year 2000 would require establishing at least one church per day. To reach the nearly three billion people who have never heard the gospel, we would have to reach one new unreached person every second of every day for the next ninety-five years— and that is not accounting for population growth! It is easy in light of this to be overawed by Satan's dominion, but we need to be impressed with who *God* is.

We serve the God of the impossible! Jesus said, "The things that are impossible with men are possible with God" and, "With God all things are possible" (Luke 18:27; Matthew 9:26). Again He promises, "All things are possible to him that believes" (Mark 9:23). We need to be consumed in prayer for the impossible task of world evangelism, praying as if it all depended on God yet working as if it all depended on us. As we respond in this way, God, in His grace, will act and we will see the task completed.

All of this, however, is dependent on us, His servants, who are saved by grace, doing everything we possibly can to get the job done. This in turn brings pleasure to the heart of God. Just as a father receives joy and responds in love to his son when he does what is asked of him, so, too, our heavenly Father receives joy and responds to us when we do what He has asked.

Jesus said, "All authority has been given to me" (Matthew 28:18). In other words, He has been given the right to rule over our lives. If we take the terms that Jesus laid down, we are bond-servants and have given up our rights. (See Romans 1:1; Philippians 1:1; James 1:1.) He is Lord over our possessions (Luke 14:33), relationships (Luke 14:26; Matthew 10:37), time (Ephesians 5:16), money—in fact over everything, and He wants our total and absolute surrender. "If Christ be God, and died for me, then no sacrifice I could make would be too great for Him," said C. T. Studd, pioneer missionary to Africa.

The Lord of the Harvest is calling us, as His children in the last days, to seek His Kingdom first and once and for all lay down the right to run our own lives. "You are not your own . . . you have been bought with a price" (1 Corinthians 6:19-20).

If Jesus Christ has authority in our lives, then He is the one calling the shots. And the last shot He called in the Bible was to "GO therefore and make disciples of all the nations" (Matthew 28:19). He is calling for an army of volunteers who will commit themselves to a lifetime of love and service for Him, the King of kings. "To know God and make Him known" should be our rallying cry as we gather at the cross ready to take on the cause for which He gave His life.

We are often told that we're "Kings Kids" and should live like princes. To this I couldn't agree more, except that there is one thing we must not forget about our King—He is at war! We need to remind ourselves of this fact daily. As long as our King is at war, we, His children, are also at war. We must become soldiers in His army and fight the enemy until that glorious day when the kingdoms of the world become the kingdoms of our Lord and of His Christ. (See Revelation 11:15.) Our daily habits and lifestyle serve as a visual demonstration to the world of how much we truly believe we are at war.

Where Are The Radicals?

Karl Marx said, "Philosophers have only interpreted the world differently; the point, however, is to change it." All over the world people are working for different causes they feel will make the world a better place. Communism is just one of those causes, and its growth worldwide is in direct relation to the number—and dedication—of its members.

In just sixty years this godless philosophy, which declares that religion is the "opiate of the masses" and that this life is all there is to live for, has taken over one third of the world. The following is an excerpt from a communist student's challenge to the church:

> The gospel is a much more powerful weapon for the renewal of society than is our Marxist philosophy, but all the same it is we who will finally beat you. . . . We communists do not play with words. We are realists, and seeing that we are determined to achieve our object, we know how to obtain the means. Of our salaries and wages we keep only what is strictly necessary, and we give up our free time and part of our holidays. You, however, give only a little time and hardly any money for the spreading of the gospel of Christ. How can anybody believe in the supreme value of this gospel if you do not practice it, if you do not spread it, and if you sacrifice neither time nor money for it. . . ? We believe in our Communist message, and we are ready to sacrifice everything, even our life. . . . But you people are afraid even to soil your hands.

We hear of student radicals, political radicals, and terrorists, but where today are the radicals for Jesus Christ? If anybody is radical, it should be us! Our Lord was the most radical person who ever lived. He spoke the most radical words, did the most radical things, and, to top it all off, rose from the dead—now *that* is radical! His disciples, too, were radicals who turned the world upside down with their message. Ten of the original twelve were martyred for their faith, and Peter and John rejoiced that they were counted worthy to suffer shame for the Lord. (See Acts 5:41.)

Church history is also filled with radicals for Christ: Polycarp singing praises to God and praying for his captors as he burned to death at the stake; Thomas Cranmer putting his hand, which had written a renunciation of Christ, into a fire and later being burned at the stake; Martin Luther, proclaiming at the Diet of Worms, when his life was threatened, "Here I stand, I can do no other—so help me God." The Reformers, Moravians, Methodists, Anabaptists, Salvation Army, and the Student Volunteer Movement were all radicals who "loved not their lives unto the death" (Revelation 12:11, *KJV*).

Many other causes both require and receive total commitment from their members in the spreading of their particular gospel. The Mormons, for example, require all their young men to spend two years on the mission field going door-to-door spreading their doctrine. Other people give their time and energy to protests against nuclear arms, wars, unfair wages, and a hundred other such causes.

How much more, then, should we who have received eternal life lay down our lives to see every kindred tongue, people, and nation share the same eternal life? How much more should we, by the power of the Spirit, be overcoming personal sin and faults so that we might walk in purity and holiness and truly shine as lights in the world? How much more should we be ready to give up the luxuries and even some of the legitimate pleasures of this life to bring joy to our heavenly Father's heart and bring eternal life and light to those who sit in darkness?

John R. Mott, the outstanding Christian leader responsible, in large part, for the founding of the Student Volunteer Movement at the turn of the century, had this challenge for his—and future—generations:

I must work the works of Him that sent me while it is day; the night cometh when no man can work. Therefore friends, in view of the awful need of men who are living tonight without Christ; in view of the infinite possibilities of the life related to Christ as mighty Saviour and risen Lord; in view of the impending crisis and urgency of the situation; in view of the conditions which favor a great onward movement within the Church of God; in view of the dangers of anything less than a great onward movement; in view of the great cloud of witnesses who gather around us, of those who subdued kingdoms and wrought righteousness—yes, in view of the constraining memories of the cross of Christ and the love wherewith He has loved us, let us rise and resolve, at whatever cost of self-denial, that live or die, we shall live or die for the evangelization of the world in our day.[1]

Evangelical Or Evangelistic?

In the last several years, some good books have been published discussing evangelicalism, and all arrive at the same conclusion: Not all evangelicals are evangelistic! Many, it seems, are evangelical in their *beliefs*—the Deity of Christ, Virgin Birth, the death and resurrection of Jesus, and so on—but few are actively seeking to *propagate their faith*.

Why is this? After all, we have the words of eternal life to give to a lost and dying world. We hold the keys to an eternity in heaven or hell. We know our obedience in spreading the faith brings great joy to the heart of God. Yet, for one reason or another we neglect to share with others and fall into the grip of either apathy or guilt for failing to do so.

Most Christians *want* to be effective in evangelism. They're not satisfied with being a secret agent Christian or silent witness. They know what the Bible says our obligations are in respect to evangelism, and they want to obey— *they simply lack understanding of how to do it.*

One day on the shore of Lake Gennesaret, Jesus helped Peter better understand the nature of evangelism—and the call He had placed on the disciple's life—by using the imagery of fishing. After helping him catch a large amount of fish, Jesus turned to Peter and said, "Do not fear, from now on you will be catching men" (Luke 5:10).

Being a fisherman, Peter knew exactly what Jesus meant, since the word He used literally means "to catch men alive." Jesus wants us to go fishing (spiritually speaking), catch men, and *bring 'em back alive!*

I believe that a great many Christians really want to be fishers of men but are frustrated by the huge gap between hearing what they should be doing and actually getting out and doing it. Recently, I stumbled upon this "Parable on Fishing" by John Drescher, and it describes well this dilemma we feel:

> "Now it came to pass that a group existed who called themselves fishermen. And lo, there were many fish in the waters all around. And the fish were hungry.
>
> "Week after week, month after month, and year after year, these, who called themselves fishermen, met in meetings and talked about their call to fish, the abundance of fish, and how they might go about fishing.

"These fishermen built large, beautiful buildings called 'Fishing Headquarters.' The plea was that everyone should be a fisherman and every fisherman should fish. One thing they didn't do, however: they didn't fish.

"Finally, after one stirring meeting on 'The Necessity for Fishing,' one young fellow left the meeting and went fishing. The next day he reported that he had caught two outstanding fish. He was honored for his excellent catch and scheduled to visit all the big meetings possible to tell how he did it. So he quit fishing in order to have time to tell other fishermen about the experience. He was also placed on the Fishermen's General Board as a person having considerable experience.

"Now it's true that many of the fishermen sacrificed and put up with all kinds of difficulties. Some lived near the water and bore the smell of dead fish every day. They received the ridicule of some who made fun of their fishermen's clubs and the fact that they claimed to be fishermen yet never fished. They wondered about those who felt it was of little use to attend the weekly meetings to talk about fishing. After all, were they not following the Master who said, 'Follow me, and I will make you fishers of men?' "

Waking The Sleeping Giant

No matter how much we talk about evangelism and our desire to bring lost men and women to faith in Christ, *talk* will not get the job done. The job will only be done when each of us goes, in obedience to Christ, and makes disciples of all nations. Are you seeing your friends, family, and neighbors evangelized? Are you witnessing to them and leading them to faith in Christ?

That's what this book is all about—crossing that gulf between hearing what we *should* be doing in evangelism and actually *doing* it. It is a practical book that will teach you how you can do it—how you can reach out to people around you, from the unreached tribes of Irian Jaya to your next door neighbor, with a gospel that is "the power of God for salvation to everyone who believes" (Romans 1:16).

I believe that within the Body of Christ today is a sleeping giant. This giant is made up of the vast majority of Christians who work in the nine-to-five workaday world and feel they don't have time to be involved in evangelism.

While talking recently with a discouraged looking brother, he said to me, "Danny, the American way of life doesn't fit too well with the Great Commission." At first I agreed with him, but as I thought about it later I began to see one of Satan's greatest lies: Christians don't think they can be effective for God in soul-winning unless they are in a *full-time* ministry or are mysteriously endued with great evangelistic gifts that enable them to leap tall buildings in a single bound!

The fact of the matter is, however, that we will be effective for God if we start to witness right where we are—on our job, at home, in our sports club, or wherever. God wants us to be faithful in little before He makes us ruler over much. (See Luke 16:10.)

Often we shy away from evangelism altogether because we have a preconceived idea—which is more often cultural than biblical—of what it takes to be effective. We think we don't really have what it takes and compare ourselves among ourselves. (See 2 Corinthians 10:12.) And all too often we come up on the short end of the stick! When we're not as eloquent as Billy Graham, as bold as Arthur Blessitt, or as flamboyant as Mario Murillo, we seek refuge behind the protective walls of our Christian community and have little contact with the world.

We need to realize that each of us is unique and special to the Lord of the Harvest, who desires to use us in His own particular way. One of Satan's greatest tricks is to keep us blinded to this. If the prince of darkness can get us to accept "superstar" theology—that evangelism is the job of a select few—then he's won a major victory over us. We must see that we are called by God, and our spiritual gifts and personalities are God-given factors that He, as the Master Potter, wants to take, shape, and mold so that we become His witnesses—His ambassadors to a lost and dying world.

Living The Lifestyle

The apostle Paul had great insight into what it takes to influence a world of unbelievers with the gospel of Jesus Christ. In his first letter to the Corinthians, Paul addressed the need for living a flexible lifestyle if he was to win men and women to a saving knowledge of God:

> And to the Jews I became as a Jew, that I might win Jews; to those who are under the Law, as under the Law, though not being myself under the Law, that I might win those who are under the Law; to those who are without law, as without law, though not being without the law of God but under the law of Christ, that I might win those who are without law. To the weak I became weak, that I might win the weak; I have become all things

to all men, that I may by all means save some. And I do all things for the sake of the gospel, that I may become a fellow partaker of it—1 Corinthians 9:20-23.

If evangelism could once again become the lifestyle for the layman of our churches and reach right to the grass roots of church life, then finishing the task would be within our reach. Michael Green has written concerning early church evangelism:

Communicating the faith was not regarded as the preserve of the very zealous or of the officially designated evangelist. Evangelism was the duty of every church member. The ordinary people of the church saw it as their job: Christianity was supremely a lay movement, spread by informal missionaries. Men will not believe that Christians have good news to share until they find that bishops and bakers, university professors and housewives, bus drivers and street corner preachers are all alike keen to pass it on, however different their methods may be.[2]

A few years ago I was having a discussion with a prospective missionary on a church-planting team about the need for a lifestyle of evangelism. He told me that although he was doing little or no outreach on his job, he would begin winning souls and discipling them when he got to the mission field. As he shared his plans, I warned him that he was going to find it difficult to witness on the mission field if he wasn't already witnessing on his job.

This young man, like many others I have met, was under the false impression that somehow, magically, automatically, he was going to become a missionary as soon as he reached the mission field. It has been said, however, that a missionary is not one who crosses the sea but one who sees the Cross! If you've seen the Cross but struggle with crossing the sea, or even the street, to tell someone about Jesus, then I pray that the following tips will help you.

Conditions For A Lifestyle Of Evangelism

1. *Get Right With God—A Pure Heart.* People in the church have a tendency to want the power of God without first having the purity of God. King David fell into this trap and couldn't properly or effectively represent God's salvation until he confessed his sin, repented, and asked God for a new start:

> Create in me a clean heart, O God; and renew a right spirit within me. Cast me not away from thy presence; and take not thy holy spirit from me. Restore unto me the joy of thy salvation; and uphold me with thy free spirit. *Then will I teach transgressors thy ways; and sinners shall be converted unto thee*—Psalm 51:10-13, *KJV, italics added.*

God desires to develop Christlike character *in us* before He ever gives us Christ-honoring fruit in our evangelism. We're told by Peter to add moral excellence to our faith, then knowledge, self-control, perseverance, godliness, brotherly kindness, and Christian love. He says, "If these qualities are yours and increasing, they render you neither useless or unfruitful in the true knowledge of our Lord Jesus Christ" (2 Peter 1:8).

In the end, we will only be effective in evangelism if the power of God is working through us. He promises to show Himself strong in behalf of those "whose heart is completely His" (2 Chronicles 16:9). That is the promise, but the *condition* is that we diligently make sure our heart is completely His, free of sin, and unspotted from the world. (See James 1:27.) God wants clean vessels doing His work, and the cleaner you are from sin and self the more He can use you—it's that simple!

2. *Get Filled With The Spirit.* "You shall receive power when the Holy Spirit has come upon you, and you shall be my witnesses in Jerusalem, and in all Judea and Samaria, and even to the remotest part of the earth" (Acts 1:8). Note that here the power was given for the express purpose of the disciples becoming witnesses.

In 1871, D. L. Moody, one of America's greatest evangelists, was preaching at a service in Chicago. As he preached, he noticed that two ladies in the front pew were busy in fervent prayer. Later, they informed him that they were praying he would receive the power of the Holy Spirit. Not long after this, Moody sensed a hunger for a deeper experience with the power of God. He describes the experience this way:

> I was crying all the time that God would fill me with His Spirit. Well, one day, in the city of New York—oh, what a day—I cannot describe it; it is almost too sacred an experience to name. I can only say God revealed Himself to me, and I had such an experience of His love that I had to ask Him to stay His hand. I went to preaching again. The sermons were not different, yet hundreds were converted. I would not now be placed back

> where I was before that blessed experience if you
> should give me all the world—it would be as the
> small dust of the balance.[3]

Regarding the gospel message he had preached to the Corinthians, Paul declared, "My preaching was not with enticing words of man's wisdom, but in demonstration of the Spirit and of power" (1 Corinthians 2:4, *KJV*). He understood how pointless it would be to try and win people from spiritual darkness to light using only carnal means. We need to allow the Holy Spirit to fill us to overflowing so our evangelism will become as effective as it possibly can be.

There are no two ways about it: If you want to be effective in evangelism, then you must be filled with God's Holy Spirit. Catherine Booth once said, "It doesn't matter how you get it, just get it!" The world that Jesus died for is at stake, so we must do God's work in His way—and that way is always Spirit-filled and Spirit-led.

3. *Get Your Priorities Straight.* Do your priorities line up with God's priorities? When people tell me they're not being effective in evangelism, I usually ask just how important winning the lost is to them. Does it play a big part in their day-to-day living?

You can easily tell what your highest priorities truly are simply by gauging how much time you spend doing various activities. How much time do you spend praying about the effectiveness of your evangelism? How often do you pray for the lost? When was the last time you prayed and fasted for someone's salvation? Do you pray for missionaries and do spiritual warfare against the forces of darkness over the world? Do you give money to gospel work and missions, and are you willing to give God more than one seventh of your week and one tenth of your money?

Allow the Holy Spirit to search your heart as you answer these questions, and seek to determine the right priority for evangelism in your life. A lost and dying world was so high on God's priority list that "He gave His only begotten Son, that whoever believes in Him should not perish, but have eternal life" (John 3:16). How high is that lost world on your priority list?

4. *Be Available.* An old preacher once said, "God is not looking for ability, but availability." When Isaiah saw the Lord's glory, he also painfully saw his own inabilities and cried out, "I am ruined! Because I am a man of unclean lips, and I live among a people of unclean lips" (Isaiah 6:5). God, however, didn't condemn him for his shortcomings but instead purged his sin and asked who was available, "Whom shall I send, and who will go for Us?" Isaiah's enthusiastic response was, "Here am I. Send me!" (Isaiah 6:8).

All too often our response goes something like, "Here I am. Send *him*!" as we point to someone we feel is more suited for the task. But there is no one else. *No one else can do exactly what you can do in your sphere of influence.* God needs ambassadors for His Kingdom in every area of life. Our response needs to be, "Lord, I'm available. Maybe I'm not much, but I'll give you all there is of me to reach a lost world. Lord, help me to bring 'em back alive."

I remember an old movie from the 1930's called, *The Green Pastures,* which portrayed how black children in the south pictured God and heaven. In one scene God asked Abraham, Isaac, and Jacob for their counsel on who would be a good candidate to deliver His children from bondage in Egypt. The trio talked it over and asked the Lord, "Does you want the brainiest or the holiest?" The Lord quickly responded, "I want the holiest; I can make him brainy!"

Although the movie had some obvious theological problems, it still portrayed an important truth. As long as we are there to present ourselves "a living and holy sacrifice, acceptable to God" (Romans 12:1), He can make us "brainy" or mold us into whatever He chooses. God chooses the foolish, base things to do His work. His army is not an army of draftees. It is made up of soldiers of the cross who are willing and available.

5. *Expect God To Use You.* Someone once said, "If you shoot an arrow and aim at nothing, then you'd better be careful; you might hit it!" Sometimes we don't expect God to use us, and we end up getting just what we expected—nothing! Hebrews 11:6 makes this clear: "Without faith it is impossible to please Him."

We need to *believe* that God will use us. The Bible promises that if we dwell in Christ, we will be fruitful: "He who abides in Me, and I in him, he bears much fruit" (John 15:5). If we abide in Christ, we should expect to bring forth fruit. William Carey, pioneer missionary to India, said, "Expect great things from God, attempt great things for God." According to Jesus, the field is ready for harvest, and all that is needed is for people simply to believe He has spoken the truth, go, and gather the harvest.

You may say, "But how could God use me?" That attitude is exactly what qualifies you for His grace; the more you realize *you* can't do it, and the less confidence you have in yourself, the more you can trust *Him* to do it through you. "Commit your way to the Lord, trust also in Him, and He will do it" (Psalm 37:5).

6. *Ask The Lord For Opportunities To Share Your Faith.* A friend of mine used to end his letters with the phrase, "Don't keep the faith—spread it." Right now, no matter where you are, you can think of unbelievers—names and faces—with whom you have regular contact. Be they relatives, fellow workers, friends, gas station attendants, or even an ice cream dipper in the park, they are all people

for whom Jesus died and who could be reached through you. Perhaps you are the only Christian contact they will ever have.

God challenges us: "Ask of Me, and I will surely give the nations as Thine inheritance, and the very ends of the earth as Thy possession" (Psalm 2:8). We need to accept this challenge, ask God for specific opportunities to share our faith with those mentioned above, and then wait expectantly.

Often the door is already open, but we have missed it by not expecting it to be. We should be like the horse at the starting gate: He is waiting—but waiting *aggressively*—for the gate to open so he can throw himself into the race. God wants us to witness for Him, and all we have to do is be ready and waiting. Then He can use us to "do exceedingly abundantly beyond all that we ask or think, according to the power that works in us" (Ephesians 3:20).

7. *Practice Personal Evangelism.* The word "practice" often sounds like a dirty word to many Christians, but lets face it: As unspiritual as it may sound, even Billy Graham didn't start out by preaching to thousands. Instead he practiced his God-given gift on much smaller groups.

We need to *develop* a lifestyle of evangelism, but, like most things in life, it takes practice. Personal evangelism is you, with all your strengths, weaknesses, idiosyncrasies, fears, and gifts sharing with someone else how they can have a relationship with the most important person in the universe—Jesus Christ.

Paul told Timothy to fan the flame of his spiritual gift and to do the work of an evangelist. (See 2 Timothy 1:6; 4:5.) You may not be an evangelist—neither was Timothy. But we are all called to be witnesses, and that requires exercising our evangelistic muscles.

I love surfing. If someone asks me to teach them to surf, the best thing I can tell them is to get on a board and try it. I could give them Nat Young's book on the history of surfing, a book on oceanography, or a subscription to Surfer magazine, but none of these would help unless they went out and tried it.

Just as you learn to surf by spending time on a board in the water, you also learn to witness by witnessing. Sure you can study the various witnessing techniques—Four Spiritual Laws, Four Facts of Life, Five Steps To Peace With God, Six Quantum Leaps to Christ!—whatever, they are all good. But they may not necessarily be *you*! When evangelism is worked into a lifestyle, then it becomes the natural outflow of what's inside you. It's spontaneous, alive, and not just a pat formula. It's "Christ in you, the hope of glory" (Colossians 1:27).

We need to practice how to open the "glory spout" and let the glory out. I can't tell you exactly how to do that because I'm not you. I can give you some principles in the following chapters that, with the Lord's help, will teach you how to touch a lost and dying land with the living water that flows out of you, but only you can decide to open up and let that water come bubbling out.

When all the principles of effective evangelism have been written, the decision to take them up and use them lies with you. Are you going to be effective in evangelism? You can be, but the choice is yours!

2

Lessons From Thessalonica

(Paul's Principles
Of Evangelism I)

CHAPTER TWO

Lessons From Thessalonica

(Paul's Principles Of Evangelism I)

In the opening verses of Acts chapter seventeen, we find the apostle Paul establishing a new church in the Macedonian city of Thessalonica. As a result of his efforts, a thriving base for the evangelization of Macedonia is founded, to which he would later address the letters of First and Second Thessalonians. Paul opens his first letter by commending the Thessalonian believers for their great evangelistic zeal, faith, hope, and love in Christ. He goes on to say that because their evangelizing had been so effective throughout the entire region, on a later visit his team had "no need to say anything" (1 Thessalonians 1:8). Now that is effective!

Paul's success in church planting at Thessalonica highlights some important principles. If we study the seventeenth chapter of Acts along with the Thessalonian epistles, we find it only took Paul three weeks to plant that church. Under the guidance of the Holy Spirit, the principles gleaned here can be used in other situations to promote effective evangelism with long lasting results. We must be careful, however, not to copy Paul's example without first having God's leading. The Holy Spirit is the one who will show us how to apply these principles in our own particular situations. "Unless the Lord builds the house, they labor in vain who build it" (Psalm 127:1).

Identification

1. *Identification In Communication.* Paul made a point of identifying with the people he was trying to reach. (See Acts 17:1.) He allowed his unbelieving audience to shape what he would say and how he would say it. Acts chapter seventeen records Paul ministering in four different locations—Thessalonica, Berea, Athens, and on Athens' Mars Hill.

In the first three instances, the apostle preached in synagogues, where he would open to Isaiah and the Psalms and show that Jesus Christ was the fulfillment of all foretold in the Jewish scriptures. He did not preach to the philosophers of Mars Hill from the Jewish scriptures, though, as these writings were unauthoritative to pagan philosophers. Instead Paul found a point of interest from which he could communicate with them. Pointing to the altar of the unknown god—an interest door through which he could share the *same* truth as he had in the synagogue—he was able to identity with the group.

Paul realized that preaching from Isaiah 53 and Psalm 22 in the Thessalonican synagogue presented the truth in a way the Jews could understand. Likewise, speaking of the creator God and quoting from their own Greek poets allowed him to identify with the philosophers on Mars Hill and help them grasp what he was saying. That's communicating!

2. *Identification In Living.* Jesus Christ is our supreme example of identification. He became one of us in order that He might reach us. In the same way, Paul explained

that he had become "all things to all men, that I may by all means save some" (1 Corinthians 9:22).

Finding the correct balance between identification with and separation from the world is not always easy. Just how far we should go is between each individual and the Lord, and we need to look continually to Him for that balance. There are instances, however, when it is necessary to step outside cultural norms.

Hudson Taylor, a young man with a burden for China, took the bold step of leaving England to live among the Chinese. Finding himself largely ineffective in sharing with the Chinese, Taylor realized the need for greater identification with the people he wanted to reach. So he began to eat Chinese food, learned the Chinese language, and grew his hair until it was long enough to braid.

Although Hudson Taylor was frowned upon by many of his contemporary missionaries and widely misunderstood at home, his results were astounding. Eventually he founded one of the most successful cross-cultural missionary movements in the history of the church—the *China Inland Mission Society*—which still thrives today as the *Overseas Missionary Fellowship*.

In 1962, Don and Carol Richardson moved to Irian Jaya as missionaries to the canabalistic, stone-aged, Sawi people. Here they found a people hardened to the gospel, among whom treachery was considered the highest virtue. When Don and Carol tried to explain the death and resurrection of Christ to the Sawi, they saw Judas as the hero of the story. His kiss of betrayal delighted them as the ultimate act of virtue.

Seeking God for an answer to their dilemma, the Richardsons discovered a cultural key that would unlock the true meaning of the gospel to the Sawi. They observed that when the Sawis made peace with another tribe, they would exchange babies as a covenant of peace. If war was declared on each other again, then each tribe would kill the other's "peace child." Don and Carol explained to the Sawi that Jesus was God's peace child whom He had sent to bring reconciliation between Himself and the world. This new perspective on the gospel resulted in hundreds of the tribe accepting the peace of Christ as they were reconciled to God. These two sensitive missionaries were able to see a major breakthrough of the gospel among the Sawi because they had identified with them and their culture.

In the late 1960's and early 70's, Chuck Smith, a pastor from a small church in Southern California called Calvary Chapel, began to feel God's burden for the hippies who were turning away from the church to drugs and the occult. As he prayed about how to reach them, God directed Lonnie Frisbee to him. Lonnie was a young, long haired evangelist with a passion for winning hippies to the Lord. God's power was tremendously demonstrated in conversions and healings. Today there are many Calvary Chapels across America, some of which have grown to include thousands in their membership. It all started when God found someone willing to identify with the people he wanted to reach.

"Jesus music" was a tool greatly used by God during this period. Innovators such as Larry Norman, Chuck Girard, and Paul Clark combined contemporary music styles with Christian lyrics in order to reach the young. In so doing, they pioneered the way for hundreds of others to use music as a point of identification with lost youth.

The Heritage Factor

Paul took advantage of many common circumstances in his evangelism. A study of his missionary journeys shows a definite and carefully planned strategy in the visits he made to various cities of the ancient world. He would go to a city, find the local synagogue, and seek to preach the gospel there. Acts 17:2 tells us this was "his custom." The synagogues contained three groups of people: Jews (natural children of Israel); Jewish proselytes (Gentiles who had joined themselves by circumcision); and God-fearers (Gentiles who believed in and feared God but who stopped short of becoming proselytes).

Often rejected and persecuted by the Jewish sector, Paul would form the nucleus of his new church from the God-fearing Gentiles, who already believed in the God of the Old Testament and needed only to be instructed in the gospel message. They were "ripe," and Paul took advantage of their scriptural heritage to reap a rich harvest of souls in the places he visited.

When Jesus spoke of the harvest field, He spoke of entering into another man's labors. (See John 4:38.) Paul understood what this meant and, as it were, harvested where the Jews had already planted the seed.

Comparing the apostle's results in Thessalonica—where there was a *heritage factor*[1] and where "many of them therefore believed, along with a number of prominent Greek women and men" (Acts 17:12)—and Mars Hill—where there was no heritage factor and only a few believed (Acts 17:35)—is very enlightening. Paul went to the religious people first, in much the same way Jesus primarily went to the Jews. (See Matthew 15:24.) The gospel was to go to Jews first, and the Gentiles would be grafted in at a later date. (See Romans 1:16 and chapter 11.)

In many nations today where significant church growth is occurring, much of the groundwork has already been done by earlier Christian workers who gave the people a heritage factor and rendered them receptive to the gospel. In Latin America, for example, it was the Catholic missionaries who laid the groundwork that has resulted in the rapid growth of the church in Brazil, Guatemala, Argentina, and other countries of the region. The same is true of the Protestant missionaries who pioneered the way for the staggering growth of the church in South Korea, Indonesia, South Africa, and even North America.

In America, 75 percent of the population claims to believe in God. Most give mental assent, at least, to the notion that Jesus was more than a man. So, having a heritage factor, we must go out, build on it, and see many won to the Lord. Studying average evangelical churches and training schools, I found that over 50 percent of those surveyed came from some type of "Christian" upbringing, be it nominally Catholic or Protestant.

I met John Pipolo one day while street witnessing, and my wife and I soon became good friends with him and his brother Anthony. They were in a sense true twentieth-century "God-fearers" from a strong Italian Catholic background. We began visiting them from time to time to share the gospel, but eventually we lost contact with each other. Other Christians, though, shared the love of Jesus with them through both personal testimony and literature. John and Anthony were encouraged to follow Jesus, and eventually they did—along with John's wife, mother, sister, and older brother. Today the Pipolo family are among some of the most committed Christians I know. Their strong Catholic heritage provided a wonderful foundation on which to build.

A common mistake made by many in their zeal to "contend earnestly for the faith" (Jude 3) is to disregard the heritage factor. In our desire to "set people straight" about their beliefs, we often end up alienating them from us.

When we attack a Roman Catholic over their belief in the mass, rosary, or the Virgin Mary, we destroy the foundation God has given us to build on in their life. We can't allow ourselves to be sidetracked from the central issue—their relationship with Jesus Christ.

I envision our witnessing as building a bridge—a relationship bridge—which will allow us to walk over the "communication gap" into the non-Christian's world and heart with the truth. The gap can be linguistic, racial, cultural, or religious, but it hinders us from communicating God's truth.

Often in attacking a person's personal beliefs, in effect we blow up the bridge God wants us to build! We should take advantage of the heritage factor and build upon it, realizing it can be a great help in conveying the truth.

Another point to keep in mind is that when we put down someone else's beliefs (for instance, an Italian, Mexican, or Filipino) they don't see it as simply a disagreement over religion but an attack on *who they are!* They are culturally "Catholic" and see themselves *born* that way. A Tibetan is *born* a Buddhist. An Indian is *born* a Hindu, etc. Eventually, of course, there will come a conflict when the truth is made clear, but I believe a key in witnessing is lifting up Jesus Christ and watching Him draw people to Himself.

In discussing the heritage factor, I am not suggesting that we attempt to reach only those with "suitable" backgrounds. There are millions of people not receptive to the gospel who have no heritage factor, and we need workers to prepare the way for them to receive the message of salvation. If, however, we are in an area that has a Christian heritage, it will be to our distinct advantage to build upon it as we share the gospel.

Consistency

Paul was consistent in his evangelism, "according to his custom" (Acts 17:2). He understood that if you sow sparingly, you will also reap sparingly, and his evangelism reflected this principle. (See 2 Corinthians 9:6.)

A farmer doesn't just sow a few seeds here and there and expect to gather in a great harvest. Instead, he prepares the ground carefully and plants a lot of seed. Likewise, no commercial fisherman will fish only when he *feels* like it but will continually let down his nets and reposition his boat until he has an adequate catch. From this we can learn an important lesson.

Evangelist Arthur Blessit tells about a young man who came to him complaining about his unfruitfulness in evangelism and wondering why Arthur was so effective in his endeavors. Arthur asked him how often he witnessed to unbelievers. "Every once in a while, as the spirit leads," was the young man's reply.

"That's the difference between you and me," Arthur responded. "I witness to almost everyone everywhere I go, and I can't imagine anyone that the Lord wouldn't want me to witness to." The fruit of his ministry speaks to the validity of this philosophy. Arthur Blessit believes in being consistent.

We must be consistent not only in planting the seed of the gospel in people's hearts but also in watering that seed. Often we give up on a person we've witnessed to because there was no immediate response. What's really needed is to build a relationship with the person. Then, over time, we are more likely to see them come to the Lord. Surveys suggest that as many as eighty percent of all converts to Christianity are the direct result of personal witness from a Christian friend.

Apologetics

The Greek word *apologia*, used several times in the New Testament, means to make a rational defense of the gospel. Paul did exactly that in his evangelism: "He went to them, and for three Sabbaths *reasoned* with them from the Scriptures, explaining and giving evidence" (Acts 17:2-3, *italics added*). The Philippians were told that Paul was "appointed for the defense [*apologia*] of the gospel" (Philippians 1:16). Likewise, Peter tells us, "Make a defense to everyone who asks you to give an account for the hope that is in you" (1 Peter 3:15).

Using apologetics in evangelism or reasoning with someone about their faith does not necessarily reveal a lack of trust in the power of God. Often it helps a person's understanding as spiritual blinders are removed. (See 2 Corinthians 4:4.)

Some say we should never defend the truth, for truth defends itself. If only that were true—but it is not. We are exhorted by Jude to "contend earnestly for the faith which was once for all delivered to the saints" (Jude 3). If we can keep our cool and reasonably disagree with a person to show them the truth, then we should take advantage of the opportunity. Remember, be sensitive to God's guiding.

I was visiting at my friend Alex's home one night when two Jehovah's Witnesses knocked at the door. Inviting them in, we began to discuss the Bible, and slowly our discussion turned into the typical Bible argument between a Christian and a Jehovah's Witness. It wasn't heated, but there were definite disagreements regarding Witness' theology and integrity of the "Watchtower" as God's prophet. After four and a half hours of reasoning, one of them, Janet, was convinced of her error and gave her life over to Jesus. She has been serving the Lord ever since.

Discussions often generate a lot of heat and little light, but, with the Spirit's guidance, we can provide people with reasons for faith in an atmosphere of love and trust and see them come to understand and know Jesus.

The most valuable apologetic tool is the Bible itself. Ample evidence for its claim to be God's Word has come from fulfilled prophecy, archeological findings, and examination of the over 24,000 manuscripts that attest to its truthfulness. Such facts can be helpful in enlightening a mind bound by spiritual darkness.

Presuppositional apologetics is also a helpful tool in this regard. With it we attempt to discover what a person believes and why they believe it. We can then draw their belief system to its logical conclusions, showing the fallacy of such a system. This is often enlightening for a non-believer because many have never thoroughly thought through what they believe. We can also contrast their belief system with one based on Biblical truth.

Keep in mind that apologetics alone will not draw a person into the Kingdom of God. Faith comes by hearing the Word of God, not reasoned arguments. (See Romans 10:17.) Apologetics' value, however, lies in the fact that, with the application of truth, we can strip away blinders from unbelieving minds held captive by Satan, thus opening the way for the light of the gospel to come in. (See 2 Corinthians 4:4.) I have witnessed and reasoned with some people who have come to see the truth of the gospel very clearly, but they still have failed to respond to it. We must not forget that it is the Holy Spirit alone—not reason—who ultimately convicts a person of their sin. (See John 16:8.)

Many books have been published on apologetics, and they are a valuable resource when seeking to communicate the gospel with a mind blinded by philosophy, ideology, tradition, a religious cult, or just plain sin. Authors such as Josh McDowell, C. S. Lewis, Francis Shaeffer, John Warwick Montgomery, and Walter Martin have all written on the subject, and the knowledge they have to share would benefit us all. Francis Shaeffer said, "We must be prepared to give honest answers to the honest questions of our generation." Apologetics allows us to do just that. "Be ready always to give an *answer* to every man" (1 Peter 3:15, *KJV, italics added*).

Simplicity—The Biblical Gospel

Paul preached the simple gospel, "explaining and giving evidence that the Christ had to suffer and rise again from the dead, and saying, 'This Jesus whom I am proclaiming to you is the Christ' " (Acts 17:3).

Despite his education, Paul did not use "persuasive words of wisdom" and determined to know nothing among the Corinthians "except Jesus Christ, and Him crucified" (1 Corinthians 2:4; 2:2). Later he warned the same church that Satan would try to lead them away from the simplicity that is in Christ. (See 2 Corinthians 11:3.)

With all our modern techniques of evangelism and apologetics, we must never forget that the preaching of the cross is the "power of God for salvation" (Romans 1:16; see also 1 Corinthians 1:18). The power of the gospel message can and has brought millions to the foot of the cross for forgiveness. So the focal point of our message, no matter how we proclaim it, must be that Jesus died on the cross for our sin and rose again from the dead. (See 1 Corinthians 15:3-4.)

Becoming a Christian is a subjective experience based upon objective truth, and we must be careful to present the

Jesus Christ of history as well as the Jesus of our experience. Christianity is true, but not just because we have personally experienced it. *It is truth whether we have experienced it or not!* If we preach solely from experience, without reference to the historical facts of Jesus' death and resurrection, we are only preaching half the truth. What happens if you backslide? Does that render the gospel untrue? No, regardless of whether or not men respond to Jesus Christ doesn't change the fact that He really did die and rise again from the dead!

Before I was a Christian, my cousin Lee and I used to take drugs together. After my conversion, I went to see him and tell him of my experience with Jesus. I explained that I didn't need drugs any more because Jesus had given me the peace and joy I longed for—He was my new "high."

Lee responded enthusiastically and told me how he had been "saved" from the drug lifestyle as well! His salvation, however, had not come from Jesus but through the Maharishi's Transcendental Meditation. As he described his newfound joy and peace, it became a battle of testimonies—my peace is better than your peace!

From that encounter I learned two important things: First, we must not communicate the gospel as though Jesus is just another experience that will get you higher than hash! Second, our testimony is *not* enough on its own. We need to share the biblical gospel and lift up the Jesus of history as well as the Jesus of our personal experience. Our testimonies are valid, even a weapon in spiritual warfare (Revelation 12:11) and should be used as the Lord leads. But we must be careful to do as Paul did and preach Jesus—crucified, buried, and risen again.

Evangelism is a proclamation of the good news to the lost. Since we know from both Scripture and experience that not all who hear are going to be saved, it cannot be defined in

terms of results. There is a difference between witnessing—
proclaiming the good news—and soul-winning—*persuad-
ing* a person to receive Christ. Because Jesus is our Lord and
has commanded us to preach the gospel to every creature,
we do—regardless of results.

Jesus does promise, however, that if we abide in Him we
will bring forth fruit. Fruit is not the issue as much as
obedience to the Lord in the proclamation of the gospel.
We can be sure we have evangelized someone if we have
faithfully proclaimed the gospel message to them. The
results then are up to God.

Preaching Amidst Opposition

Paul preached despite opposition: "The Jews, becoming
jealous and taking along some wicked men from the market place, formed a mob and set the city in an uproar" (Acts
17:5).

Wherever Paul went there was either a revival or a riot!
Yet he didn't let it slow him down because he knew from
the beginning of his call to preach that he would suffer
persecution. (See Acts 9:16.) He knew that chains and
afflictions were waiting for him in every city, but his
response was,

> None of these things move me, neither count
> I my life dear unto myself, that I might finish my
> course with joy, and the ministry, which I have
> received of the Lord Jesus, to testify the gospel of
> the grace of God—Acts 20:23-24, *KJV.*

The New Testament is full of promises that believers are
called to suffer for the gospel's sake. (See Matthew 5:11,

10:22, 13:21; Romans 8:17, 36; 2 Corinthians 1:7; Philippians 1:29; 2 Timothy 2:12; and 1 Peter 5:10.) Of course, these aren't the kind of promises that we see sold in the promise boxes in Bible bookstores, but they are nonetheless promises.

Rather than regarding persecution and opposition to the gospel as uncommon intruders into our work, we should see these hard situations as an opportunity for God to show His greatness on our behalf. Whether His will is to deliver us *from* the trial or deliver us *in* the trial is His business; our responsibility is to be faithful to Him as He works "all things together for good" (Romans 8:28).

Second Timothy 2:12 promises, "If we endure [suffer], we shall also reign with Him." You should never go looking for persecution (unless you're a masochist!), but when it comes, you don't have to stop doing the work. Some Christians give up evangelizing because they encounter opposition in their work. Remember, there is a war going on, and Satan will do anything he can to hinder the progress of the gospel.

When we live as God wants us to, the devil will get angry! "All who desire to live godly in Christ Jesus will be persecuted" (2 Timothy 3:12). Once we purpose to live or die for the evangelization of the world, we will draw Satan's attacks, as honey attracts bees. Satan is after those who pose a threat to his kingdom, but Jesus is the victor. Hallelujah! We need not fear.

Scripture tells us to stand against the schemes of the devil. (See Ephesians 6:11.) Satan is crafty in his attacks on God's children, using any and every means to stop our effectiveness. Sometimes he comes like a lion—perhaps a Muslim fanatic trying to kill us. At other times he'll appear as an angel of light, bringing a false doctrine that tickles our ears and appeals to the flesh. (See 2 Corinthians 11:14.) Other times he uses well-meaning Christians who exhort us to experience the "good life" of health and wealth, while we miss God's call for our life.

Don't be ignorant of Satan's devices. (See 2 Corinthians 2:1.) Opposition in evangelism comes simply because we are seeking to set spiritual prisoners free, and Satan won't let them go easily! (See 2 Timothy 2:26.)

In addition to Satan's opposition, we will also experience human opposition! People don't like to be told they need to change—selfish people don't enjoy being challenged to deny themselves. Galatians 5:11 tells us there is a built-in offense to the gospel message. When it is preached with power, it stirs reactions that range from total acceptance to apathy, indifference, and outright persecution. We must be prepared for this and not allow any type of persecution to deter us.

Solomon warns, "The sluggard will not plow by reason of the cold; therefore shall he beg in harvest, and have nothing" (Proverbs 20:4). We cannot allow the "cold" of opposition to hinder our work in God's harvest field. Instead, we must purpose in our hearts to be committed to His work. Only by doing Christ's will can we bring pleasure to His heart.

> And though the earth with devils filled
> Will threaten to undo us,
> We will not fear for God hath willed
> His truth to triumph through us.
> Let goods and kindred go,
> This mortal life also.
> The body they may kill;
> God's truth abideth still
> And we must win the battle.
> —Martin Luther

Kingdom Preaching

Paul preached the Kingdom of God:

> And . . . they began dragging Jason and some
> brethren before the city authorities, shouting,
> "These men who have upset the world have come
> here also . . . saying that there is another king,
> Jesus"—Acts 17:6-7.

Paul and his team "turned the world upside down" (verse
6, *KJV*) by preaching that Jesus was King and rightful ruler
over all the earth. They didn't see Jesus as an optional extra
to be added to the pantheon of gods but proclaimed Him
as the Divine Sovereign with the right to rule over people's
lives.

The early church had a theological basis for the aggressive evangelism with which they turned the world upside
down. Their watch word was, "Jesus is Lord." He *is* King
and desires to bring His rule and reign to this earth: "Thy
Kingdom come. Thy will be done, on earth as it is in heaven"
(Matthew 6:10).

Understanding this will help us to be bold in our evangelism. We are not a people groveling in the dirt of the devil's
world, begging others to accept Jesus as their "personal
Savior." Rather, we are a people who realize, "The earth is
the Lord's, and all it contains, the world and all who dwell
in it" (Psalm 24:1).

We have been given a mandate—"The kingdom of God
is at hand: repent ye, and believe the gospel" (Mark 1:15,
KJV)—and don't need to be intimidated by people as we witness. After all, we not only have the responsibility but the
right to carry out the work of evangelism because of the
authority of Him who has commanded us to do so.

The fullness of the Kingdom of God will not come until Jesus returns, but the church *here and now* must seek to establish Christ's reign in every area of life. We must be a prophetic voice against evil and injustice. The plight of the poor and murder of the unborn, for example, should be of serious concern to us who represent the King. We are to be the salt of the earth, as well as the light of the world. (See Matthew 5:13-14.) The presence of the Kingdom of God should be a restraining force (salt) against the evil of this world while at the same time being a positive force for good (light).

The educational system needs Kingdom teachers and students who can uphold the banner of righteousness and make a stand against humanism. Countries need politicians who will lead the people of God, implementing His principles of justice and righteousness in secular government. The sports world, too, needs heros that can point to the King rather than drugs as the source of their strength. The world also desperately needs to see Christian marriages and families that are a representation of Christ's love for the Church.

The Church is the expression of the Kingdom of God on earth. Our personal holiness, love for one another, concern over the poor and social issues, commitment to missions, and even our physical lifestyle must all be a reflection of Him. When we put His Kingdom first, everything else falls into its proper place. (See Matthew 6:33.)

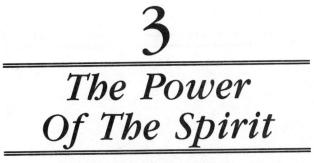

3

The Power Of The Spirit

(Paul's Principles
Of Evangelism II)

CHAPTER THREE

The Power Of The Spirit

(Paul's Principles Of Evangelism II)

Shortly after Paul was forced to flee the persecution in Thessalonica, he sent Timothy back to see how the infant church was doing. Timothy's report was full of "good tidings of [their] faith and love" (1 Thessalonians 3:6). The apostle then wrote his first epistle to the Thessalonians, from which we can glean more principles of evangelism. Using these principles, Paul pioneered one of the most fruitful of all the early churches.

The Futility Of Man's Wisdom

Paul preached in the power of God: "For our gospel did not come to you in word only, but also in power and in the Holy Spirit and with full conviction" (1 Thessalonians 1:5). He understood that the message itself was powerful. (See Romans 1:16.) But he also knew that words alone weren't sufficient to draw blinded minds and hardened hearts to the Lord Jesus Christ unless God, by His Spirit, first put His power on those words. Paul informed the intellectual Greeks of Corinth,

> My message and my preaching were not in persuasive words of [man's] wisdom, but in demonstration of the Spirit and of power, that your faith should not rest on the wisdom of man, but on the power of God—1 Corinthians 2:4-5.

Paul resisted the temptation to rely on his own abilities and relied instead on the power of God to bear witness of the word that was preached with "signs and wonders and by various miracles and by gifts of the Holy Spirit" (Hebrews 2:4).

God reminded Zerubbabel, " 'Not by might nor by power, but by My Spirit,' says the Lord of Hosts" (Zechariah 4:6). God designed evangelism in such a way that He *won't* do it without us, and we *can't* do it without Him. He is quick to withdraw His hand from our work when we trust in human methods or gimmicks that are devoid of His Spirit, letting us come to the end of our rope so we will cry out to Him for His power and anointing. The Lord wants us to see that there is no substitute in evangelism for His power. More can be accomplished in a few weeks of ministry in the power of God than through years of powerless preaching.

Shortly after the turn of the century, evangelist John G. Lake answered God's call to the mission field of South Africa. After much preaching without seeing any results, he began to fast and pray. On the twenty-first day of his fast, as the evangelist walked down a street in Johannesburg, he noticed a horse with a broken leg. A policeman held his gun poised ready to put it out of its misery. Lake quickly stretched out his hand and prayed for the animal, which was instantly healed and got up and went its way. From that point on, Lake saw a new church established in South Africa on the average of one every three days![1]

In his book, *Thy God Reigneth*, R. Edward Miller tells the story of a powerful visitation of the Holy Spirit in Argentina during 1954. After two and a half years of patient prayer and waiting on God by a group of intercessors, He poured out His Spirit.

> Up until that time, the evangelical works were limited. Most of the churches were comparatively small; conversions were here and there; and healings were few. Who could imagine that God would move out on a large scale when He had never done it before![2]

Miller goes on to tell how a little known American evangelist named Tommy Hicks came to Argentina, in obedience to the Spirit's leading, to hold an evangelistic healing campaign. Hicks went to see President Peron and was stopped at the palace door by an armed guard. He prayed for the guard and saw him instantly healed. The next day that guard escorted him to see the President.

Peron suffered from eczema, which no physician seemed able to cure. The disease had progressed to the point where Peron allowed no photographs of him to be taken. Hicks prayed for the President, and he, too, was healed instantly. This opened the way for a two-month salvation and healing campaign, which, at its peak, had over 200,000 people in attendance. Many people were saved and healed of incurable sicknesses and diseases. The Lord confirmed His Word with His power.

Indonesia, too, has experienced a mighty baptism in the power of God in recent years. Mel Tari describes the outpouring in the book, *Like A Mighty Wind*. The preaching of the gospel, accompanied by signs and wonders, has contributed significantly to the phenomenal growth of the church in Indonesia since 1966. On the island of Timor alone, the Evangelical Christian Church grew by 100,000 members in only four years. While other factors have helped contribute to this influx, Christianity has gained over two and a half million converts in Muslim Indonesia since 1965.

Fighting Fire With Fire

Anyone who has been to the mission field and observed the powers of darkness at work in spiritism, witchcraft, and false religions would agree that for a significant end-time harvest we will need to see a corresponding display of the power of God through signs and wonders. Whenever a display of satanic power occurs, the darkness needs to be countered with a greater display of the power of God. (See Exodus 7:10-13; Acts 13:6-12; 16:16-18; 1 John 4:4.) "When the enemy shall come in like a flood, the Spirit of the Lord shall lift up a standard against him" (Isaiah 59:19, *KJV*).

We see this demonstrated over and over in the New Testament. The Samaritans were "giving attention to what was said by Philip, as they *heard and saw the signs which he was performing*" (Acts 8:6, *italics added*). When Peter spoke the word of faith to heal Aeneas, "All who lived at Lydda and Sharon saw him, and they turned to the Lord" (Acts 9:33-35). As word got around Joppa that Peter had raised Dorcas from the dead, "many believed in the Lord" (Acts 9:42). Sergius Paulas, the deputy, got saved after seeing Elymas the sorcerer blinded by Paul. (See Acts 13:11-12.) After Jesus healed the nobleman's son, the whole family immediately believed in Him. (See John 4:47-53.)

Perhaps the most effective way to begin moving in this "supernatural evangelism" is to step out and exercise our spiritual gifts—right out among non-Christians. Jesus exercised both the word of wisdom and the word of knowledge when dealing with the woman at the well. (See John 4:1-42.) The Lord relied on supernatural wisdom and used the interest door of living water. He also knew the perfect time to speak the word of knowledge He had received from His Father regarding her previous five husbands and present live-in boyfriend.

Proverbs 11:30 tells us that it takes wisdom to win souls. As we seek God, He will at times give us divine information regarding situations so we can effectively move in supernatural power.

Recently, several friends and I decided to have an impromptu time of street evangelism. We gathered for our usual pre-outreach prayer time, and some felt impressed by the Lord not to go out witnessing but to stay back and pray for the others.

I was one of those who went out witnessing. After an uneventful hour or so, I approached a young man in the doorway of a bar. Within several minutes of conversation with Cliff, I found he wasn't a Christian, but he was open and ready to receive. I felt distinctly impressed by the Lord to "press" him for a decision. I'm usually hesitant to do that because I don't want to talk anyone into something someone else can talk them out of! This time, though, I felt I needed not only to *proclaim* but also to *persuade*. After a couple of hours, Cliff was gloriously saved; he is still walking with the Lord.

I did not know it at the time, but back at the prayer meeting, Christopher, one of the leaders, had received a vision of a young man in a green shirt who was ready to receive and needed to be pressed for a commitment to Christ. In direct response to their intercession, I was able to be sensitive to Cliff's need and lead him to salvation. He was wearing a green shirt, too!

The next week we used the same strategy, and this time I felt led to stay back and pray. In the time of intercession, God impressed upon me the story of the prodigal son (Luke 15), so we proceeded to pray specifically that God would use our team to bring prodigal sons home. That night two backsliders recommitted their lives to Christ.

Often the Lord will give believers a word of knowledge about someone who will help break down their resistance to the gospel. For example, Marty, a surfer and lifeguard at a local beach, was a backslidden Christian who had gotten involved with the occult. A *Youth With A Mission (YWAM)* summer outreach team was witnessing on the beach, and one of the participants approached Marty with a gospel tract. The young evangelist was met with cold rejection.

The next day, as the outreach team prayed in preparation for their day's witnessing at a local shopping mall, God impressed upon them that they should go back instead to the beach where they were the day before. As they approached the beach, God gave several words of knowledge to Dave, one of the team members, about Marty's past life.

Dave approached Marty and told him facts about his previous conversion, involvement in the occult, and other specifics about his life, which Dave had no way of knowing in the natural. Then he invited Marty to the *YWAM* base to meet me since we had a similar cultural background. Marty gave his life back to the Lord that night, and within a year and a half he was working as a medical missionary among the poor of the Philippines. But it took a work of the supernatural to open him up to the truth.

God also demonstrates His power by convicting unbelievers of their sin. (See John 16:8.) Paul told the Thessalonians that the gospel was preached "in the Holy

Spirit and with full conviction" (1 Thessalonians 1:5). Only the Holy Spirit can convict a person of their sin and show them their need of Jesus for salvation. They must be convicted and convinced they are lost before they will ever want to be saved. We must allow the Spirit to do His convicting work in a person's heart before we persuade them to receive Jesus.

Peter's pentecostal sermon illustrates the workings of the human and divine elements in evangelism. Peter *proclaimed* the gospel message, and then his hearers were pierced to the heart and asked Peter and the apostles what they needed to do. (See Acts 2:37.) After seeing evidence of the Spirit's convicting work, Peter *persuaded* them to receive Jesus. Proclamation, conviction, and then persuasion—in that order.

J. Edwin Orr, authority on evangelical awakenings, states that one of the common elements in great revivals of the past is a deep conviction of sin—first in the church, and then in the world. The late Duncan Cambell described men under conviction during the Hebrides revival crying out for mercy, saying, "Hell is too good for me, hell is too good for me."

According to accounts of revivalist preaching of the eighteenth and nineteenth centuries, people would cry out to God, shrieking, groaning, and sometimes even falling unconscious under the conviction of sin! Before the good news can be received, the bad news first must be believed. That is, sinners must know they are separated from God. Only then will they seek to be saved from their sin.

We need the power of God upon us as we evangelize. And we must be prepared to do God's work in God's way, leaving the results to Him. As we carry on the Great Commission, we must seek God continually for His power to be upon us in anointed preaching, signs and wonders, conviction of sin, and holy living.

Awareness Of Hell

First Thessalonians 1:10 makes it clear that the apostle Paul was aware of hell: "Jesus, who delivered us from the wrath to come."

Hell is never pleasant to discuss, but its reality is spelled out over and over as we search the New Testament. Jesus spoke often of an eternal abode of the lost, warning of its danger and describing it as a place of "everlasting punishment" and "outer darkness," where there is "weeping and gnashing of teeth" (Matthew 25:46; 8:12).

Peter spoke also of a "mist of darkness . . . reserved forever" for false teachers, and Jude spoke of the "blackness of darkness for ever" (2 Peter 2:17; Jude 13, *KJV*). In light of such descriptions, it would be well for us to meditate on the subject of hell and allow God to break our hearts with the very thing that breaks His heart—the thousands of souls that pass every day into a Christless eternity.

Charles Spurgeon, the "Prince of Preachers," is not known for his hell-fire sermons, but in one instance he sought to bring a greater awareness of hell to his hearers:

> "Your body will be prepared by God in such a way that it will burn forever without being consumed. With your nerves laid raw by the searing flame, yet never desensitized for all its raging fury and acrid smoke of the sulfureous flames searing your lungs and choking your breath, you will cry out for mercy of death but it will never, no never, no never give you surcease."[3]

Whether or not Spurgeon's opinion is literally true doesn't matter, but it should awaken us to the fact that the Bible depicts hell as a place of eternal torment. Descriptions such as "outer darkness" and "black darkness" should fill us with a sense of fear for those who are on their way to such a place.

All of us, at some time or another, have been afraid of the dark. Imagine, though, the torment for someone who, in total darkness, remembers his lifetime and all the beautiful sights he has seen—the flowers, the sunsets, the pretty faces, and so many other things that come flooding back. (See Luke 16:25.) He remembers the good times, the bad times, and the times he had the opportunity to receive Christ but rejected Him. He realizes that for the rest of *eternity* he will continue to see nothing but darkness and have nothing to look forward to—nothing but reflecting on his own foolishness in not accepting Christ.

It is said that William Booth, founder of the Salvation Army, wished all his officers could hang over hell for twenty-four hours prior to their commissioning. He felt sure this would stir in them a deeper commitment to evangelism. While a greater awareness of hell should not be our primary motive for evangelism, knowing we are delivered from the wrath to come should have a definite place in our theology of missions.

A Matter Of Life And Death

I believe that our supreme motive in reaching the lost should be our love for the Lord and a desire to please Him. But we also need a revelation of the lostness of the lost. We need to ask ourselves continually whether we truly believe our friends, relatives, and acquaintances, as well as the heathen, are forever lost unless they turn to Christ. The fact that God in His infinite wisdom has laid down a just penalty for sin—eternal separation from Him and His life—should motivate us to reach out and love our neighbor as ourself by sharing the gospel message with them.

The advent of different forms of liberal and modernistic theology has seen the subject of hell slowly lose its sting. Apart from the occasional reference to Jonathan Edwards' "Sinners in the Hands of an Angry God" or a thumping hell-fire and brimstone message from a Southern Baptist, hell is seldom mentioned from the pulpit. Nowadays, it is most often used as a swear word or in jest in careless remarks like, "When I get to hell, I'll throw a party because so many of my friends will be there." Rather than allowing people to make light of such an awful place, we must tell them the folly of their way, being prepared even to weep in front of them, if need be, to show them the gravity of the issue.

Leonard Ravenhill tells of Charlie Peace, a convicted criminal sentenced to die by hanging. On his death-walk to the gallows, the prison chaplain glibly read him some Bible verses from a book called, "The Consolation of Religion." Charlie was shocked that a minister who professed to believe in the Bible could so coldly and professionally read about hell without so much as a tear in his eye or a quiver in his voice.

How can he believe that there is an eternal fire that never consumes its victims and yet be so unmoved? Charlie mused to himself. Finally, unable to hold his peace any longer, the convict snapped at the chaplain, "Sir, if I believed what you and the church of God say you believe, even if England were covered with broken glass from coast to coast, I would walk over it, if need be, on hands and knees, and think it worthwhile living, just to save one soul from an eternal hell like that."

As I heard Leonard Ravenhill share this, I was cut to the heart and felt the Holy Spirit challenging me with, "Danny, how much do you really believe in the gospel?"

Paul said he had the "spirit of faith, according to what is written, 'I believed, therefore I spoke,' we also believe, therefore also we speak" (2 Corinthians 4:13). It follows, then, that if we truly believe the gospel is God's absolute final word to mankind regarding salvation, our only right response should be to get the news out—by every means possible.

Leighton Ford tells of a European communist who remarked that the only Christian he respected was the one trying to convert him to Christ. We, who are persuaded, need also to be *persuaders*!

The work of evangelism is serious business. We are not just trying to give people a new lease on this life by joining our religion, we are dealing with the issues of life and death—heaven and hell—every time we encounter a non-believer. Paul spoke of having unceasing grief in his heart and wishing he were accursed from Christ for the sake of the lost. (See Romans 9:2-3.) The Psalmist also agonized in his concern for the lost: "Horror hath taken hold upon me because of the wicked that forsake thy law. . . . Rivers of waters run down mine eyes" (Psalm 119:53, 136, *KJV*). Jeremiah spoke of sobbing in secret and bitterly weeping over the pride of his people. (See Jeremiah 13:17.)

Many of us find such statements eccentric and extreme, but how can we say they are extreme in light of the reality of hell? If only God would give us half the revelation of the lostness of the lost that these men had, we would be led to fasting, prayer, spiritual warfare, giving, and fearless witnessing to see the lost come to Jesus and escape the dangers of a Christless eternity.

After declaring that we all must stand before the judgment seat of Christ, Paul says, "Knowing the terror of the Lord, we persuade men" (2 Corinthians 5:11, *KJV*). It is not so much that we need to incorporate hell more into our witnessing, although that may be appropriate at times; rather we Christians, who know the "terror of the Lord," should be motivated to persuade men.

The evangelistic messages of Acts are strangely silent regarding hell (and heaven, for that matter). I believe this is because God doesn't want us to use tactics of fear and threat to scare people into salvation any more than He wants us to use "pie in the sky" to bribe them. Instead, He wants us to present the truth of His death and resurrection that will set men free. (See 1 Corinthians 15:3-4.) The eternal issue of heaven and hell needs mostly to be pressed on *our* minds, as Christians, *so that we see* the gravity and urgency of the matter.

True Repentance

Paul preached repentance: "You turned to God from idols to serve a living and true God" (1 Thessalonians 1:9).

The apostle understood that becoming a Christian was not just giving "mental assent" to a set of theological creeds. It meant turning away *from* sin and idolatry (repentance) *to* Jesus Christ (faith). Paul summarized this in his letter to the Ephesian elders: " . . . repentance toward God and faith in our Lord Jesus Christ" (Acts 20:21).

Repentance is the first word of the gospel. Jesus said, "Repent and believe in the gospel" (Mark 1:15). He made it clear that His reason for coming was to preach repentance. (See Luke 5:32.) Likewise, He commands us to preach it as well. (See Luke 24:47.)

True repentance is the natural outworking of true faith. Jesus linked the two very closely when He said the Ninevites had "repented at the preaching of Jonah" (Luke 11:32). The account in the book of Jonah, however, records that they "believed in God" and makes no specific mention of repentance (Jonah 3:5). By inference, we can conclude that repentance and faith are very closely linked, and we dare not separate them. The call to faith and the call to repentance are one and the same.

In 1981, two Christians, one an Indian and the other a Chinese *YWAM*er, knocked at a devout young Hindu woman's door. After being invited in, they noticed idols everywhere. Undeterred, Sam Yeo Le Hok began sharing both his testimony and the gospel. Sashikala, the young Hindu woman, was soon asking what she needed to do to receive salvation, and the two patiently explained her need to repent of sin and receive Christ as her Savior and Lord. Sashikala understood and was willing to pay the price to follow Jesus completely. Soon a bonfire raged in the backyard as the Hindu deities Shiva, Hanuman, Krishna, along with other idols, were burned.

Dietrich Bonhoeffer, the German theologian, warned of the dangers of offering cheap grace. He has this to say about the price God places on His grace:

> Such grace is costly because it cost a man his life, and it is grace because it gives him the only true life. It is costly because it condemns sin, and grace because it justifies the sinner. Above all, it is costly because it cost God the life of His son. "Ye are bought with a price," and what has cost God so much, cannot be cheap for us.[4]

In our witnessing, we must be careful not to compromise the gospel message for the sake of increased numbers of converts. This can happen when we neglect to preach repentance. By watering down the gospel, we can rob a prospective convert of the joy of sins forgiven. Peter said, "Repent ye therefore, and be converted, that your sins may be blotted out" (Acts 3:19, *KJV*)

If we turn away from sin, take up our cross, and follow Jesus, He demonstrates His power to us by giving victory over our sin. That, in turn, glorifies Him. But we rob our hearers of the joy of victorious Christian living when we neglect to give them the full gospel. It is true that there will be struggles with besetting sin, but as our heart and will is set to follow Jesus, we soon become victorious.

A word of caution should be added here regarding legalism. We must see ourselves as a friend to a new convert, helping him walk out his repentance *from what the Bible says is sin*, not trying to mold him to the standards and beliefs of our particular denomination or group. We all have a certain "grid," formed by our particular cultural and denominational environment, through which we view those "gray areas" that the Bible is silent about. We must be careful, however, not to impose our "grid" on new converts in place of true biblical repentance, thereby ensnaring them in a web of legalism. Each new Christian needs space to develop their own "grid," which is done as they individually seek God and study His Word. We must be careful not to preach the doctrines of men in place of the commandments of God. (See Matthew 15:9.)

The bottom line in all of this is that the gospel is not man-centered but God-centered. It does not revolve around the happiness of man but the glory of God. Jesus is not just a personal Savior who will meet people's needs. He is not some sugar-daddy in the sky, a cosmic butler who responds to our every whim, a washing powder that washes whiter, or a trip to end all trips. *Jesus Christ is the Lord of the Universe and demands our full surrender.* Without Christ, man is an unfortunate creature that God is not obligated to save. By his wicked works man has made himself an enemy of God and is under the guilt of his sin. (See Colossians 1:21.) Man deserves judgment, but by God's mercy and grace, through repentance, he can be forgiven.

Loving Sinners

If we do not have God's love for the lost, then any evangelistic methods or principles we use will at best be legalistic, stale obedience to a set of commands. The "agape" love of God needs to be the foundation upon which our evangelism is based.

> Having thus a fond affection for you, we were well-pleased to impart to you not only the gospel of God but also our own lives, because you had become very dear to us—1 Thessalonians 2:8.

Paul told us that even if he abounded in faith, knowledge, spiritual gifts, and good works, but did not have love, then it was all worth nothing. (See 1 Corinthians 13:1-3.) Jesus said that all men would know we are His disciples by the love we have for each other. (See John 13:34-35.) We must be diligent to make sure that is indeed the case. Christians should not be the sole recipients of our love, however, but also those who desperately need it—the unbelievers: "And may the Lord cause you to increase and abound in love (agape) for one another and *for all men*" (1 Thessalonians 3:12, *italics added*).

When speaking of love, I am not referring to some type of emotional sentimentality or a special way of feeling. God's love is a *choice*—choosing the highest good of another regardless of our personal feelings. God's feelings toward sinners are recorded in Psalm 7:11: "God is angry with the wicked every day," but He "commendeth his love towards us" (Romans 5:8, *KJV*).

God chose our highest good above His own feelings. His loving, merciful response to our sin was the Cross. There are times when unbelievers will not elicit great feelings of love from us, as they blaspheme the Lord and reject or persecute us. But even in these situations we must choose to be Christlike and love them regardless of their actions.

An illustration of this kind of love is found in David Wilkerson's book, *The Cross and the Switchblade.* Nicky Cruz, a young gang member, threatened to cut David into a thousand pieces. David's response was one of agape love: "You cut me into a thousand pieces and every piece will say, 'I love you.'" Soon afterwards, Nicky was converted. He has gone on to preach Christ's love to thousands more.

The fruit of a Spirit-filled life is God's love pouring out of us to whomever we come in contact with in the course of our day, be they Christian or non-Christian. (See Galatians 5:22.) We need to be filled with the Holy Spirit regularly, especially when evangelizing. Before approaching someone, we need to ask for God's help in truly loving that person. We will be tested at times, but during those times we grow in our capacity to love with God's unconditional love. (See Matthew 5:43-48.)

As a new Christian, barely a week old in my faith, my love for the unsaved was severely tested. Working as a dishwasher in a restaurant, I witnessed to the other employees. One of them, John, the cook, was a member of the church of Satan. As I told him about the gospel and the second coming of Jesus Christ, he looked at me with evil in his eyes and let loose a series of blasphemy against the Lord. One thing he said was, "If Jesus Christ came back to earth right now and walked into this restaurant, I'd hit him on the head with an axe and pick the worms out of his brain."

Speechless, I fell back against the dishwashing machine. I couldn't believe anyone could say such foul and demonic things about God. In my silence, the Holy Spirit whispered to me, "Danny, do you still love him?" I had to be honest; in my heart I knew I didn't. The Lord knew it, too, and responded with, "I do!"

That day I learned an important lesson: When someone is unlovely—and John was about as unlovely as you could get—God can give us His love for that person. I felt like hitting John with an axe, but God showed me the love He had for him. I wish I could report that John got saved, but I don't know if he ever did. But I do know that God is still commending His love toward sinners just like John, and, if we are going to follow in the footsteps of our Master, we must do the same.

Light Shining Evangelism

Paul was a living example of what he preached: "You also became imitators of us and of the Lord" (1 Thessalonians 1:6).

Jesus spoke of what I call "light shining evangelism" in His Sermon on the Mount. He instructed us to let men see our good works so they in turn will glorify the Father in heaven. (See Matthew 5:16.) Often, simply doing a good work for a non-Christian will open them to the gospel. (See Titus 2:14.) Helping a neighbor by painting his house, cutting his lawn, or even baby-sitting his children can open his eyes to the "Light of the World."

> That ye may be blameless and harmless, sons
> of God, without rebuke, in the midst of a crooked
> and perverse nation, *among whom ye shine as
> lights in the world*; holding forth the word of
> life—Philippians 2:15-16.

Paul was confident his own life reflected the message
he preached. He did not preach unobtainable theories but
invited people to see them worked out in his own life,
confident that he displayed significant victory over the
world, the flesh, and the devil. Thus he could boldly tell
the Thessalonians, "Follow me" (2 Thessalonians 3:7).

A Christlike example is essential if we are to be effective
in evangelism. I have interviewed scores of people who have
been brought to salvation simply by seeing the gospel lived
out in a person's life. Charles Finney once said, "Christians
are the greatest reason for accepting Christ; they are also
the greatest excuse not to." Just as "the Word became flesh,
and dwelt among us" (John 1:14), so today that Word must
be lived out in the lives of those who are His Body.

Unfortunately, the bumper sticker, "Christians aren't
perfect, just forgiven," seems to describe more adequately
the gospel as we represent it to the world. In a technical
sense it is true that none of us are sinlessly perfect, but the
New Testament also teaches that we are more than just
forgiven. It teaches that we are forgiven *and changed*. Jesus
died not only to bring forgiveness *of* sin but also victory
over sin. (See Romans 6.)

By God's grace we can "cleanse ourselves from all defile-
ment of flesh and spirit, perfecting holiness in the fear of
God" (2 Corinthians 7:1). We are partakers of His holiness
and divine nature. (See Hebrew 12:10; 2 Peter 1:4.) And we
have been promised that, as a result of the New Covenant,
He will give us the power of His Spirit to live and walk

victoriously as we obey Him. "I will put My Spirit within you and cause you to walk in My statutes, and you will be careful to observe My ordinances" (Ezekiel 36:27).

I can't imagine Paul sheepishly walking up to a fellow tentmaker, head down, and saying, "I'm just as much a creep as you are, but I'm forgiven. Don't look at me—look at Jesus!" No, I think he would have witnessed something like this: "I was a creep, but Jesus forgave me and changed my life. He gives me power over the world, the flesh, and the devil because He gave me His Holy Spirit. Follow me because I'm following Jesus." Rather than revealing pride in saying this, he would instead be giving God the glory for the changes worked in his life. As the song says, "From glory to glory He's changing me, His likeness and image made perfect in me."

Not all of us are Pauls, and the thought of going up to someone we have never met and sharing the gospel with them strikes fear and dread to our heart. When confronted with the challenge of a lifestyle of evangelism, our reply is, "Well, that's okay for them because they're so outgoing," or, "Yeah, I'd like to, but it's just not me. I could never be as bold as that." Our reaction, however, doesn't need to be that way—the nagging fears and doubts *can* be overcome.

4

Fears And Attitudes

CHAPTER FOUR

Fears And Attitudes

"Paranoia strikes deep; into your life it will creep; it starts when you're always afraid . . . "

Although the words quoted above were penned by a secular rock musician, they accurately describe the number one hindrance to the lifestyle of evangelism—the fear of man. Proverbs 29:25 warns, "The fear of man brings a snare." I'm sure each one of us would admit that, at some time or other, this fear has ensnared our witnessing for the Lord.

There have been times when I felt frustrated and frightened when God led me to witness to someone. In the face of scriptural admonitions to fear not—"perfect love casts out fear" (1 John 4:18)—one way or another fear seemed to cast out my perfect love! There were times when I tried to be God's man of faith and power, mustering my courage and willpower; but, when it came to opening my mouth and witnessing, I simply chickened out.

The Lord began to speak to me about how to deal with specific fears in the light of His Word. Let's look at some of the most common fears I have discovered, both from my own experience and from interviewing other Christians in many parts of the world.

1. *Fear Of Rejection.* This is a big fear, especially in the western world. Rejection is hard to handle, even for the most

75

thick-skinned of us, because we have a built-in need for love and acceptance. In witnessing, though, we often find people neither loving nor accepting, so we must face this fact: *Every ambassador for Christ is essentially a rejected person!*

Jesus was "despised and rejected of men" (Isaiah 53:3, *KJV*). "He came to His own, and those who were His own did not receive Him" (John 1:11). "They rose up and cast Him out of the city" (Luke 4:29). "And when they saw Him, they entreated Him to depart from their region" (Matthew 8:34). "He must suffer many things and be rejected by this generation" (Luke 17:25). Many accepted Jesus and His message, but more still rejected Him. If we want to be like Him, we must learn to handle this same rejection.

When I teach on evangelism, I like to ask, "Do you feel like witnessing on the streets tonight?" Usually, only a small percentage raises their hands, so I continue, "What if I guarantee that tonight each one of you will lead the first person you approach to the Lord—how many would feel like it then?" Almost without fail, every hand will shoot up. Everyone wants themselves and their message to be accepted. No one relishes being put down, ignored, or looked upon as a fool.

The key to handling rejection is making sure we are getting all the acceptance we need from the Father and not looking for it in the world. By its very nature, evangelism means we are uninvited people taking an uncomfortable message to a Christ-rejecting world where many will refuse it. The glorious good news is, however, that some will accept it if we go out fearlessly, trusting that the perfect love of Jesus will cast out fear.

Scripture tells us, "In the fear of the Lord there is strong confidence, and his children shall have refuge. The fear of the Lord is a fountain of life, that one may avoid the snares of death'' (Proverbs 14:26-27). If we look to the Lord for our acceptance, placing our identity in Him and standing in awe of who He is, then the snare of the fear of man will fall away.

Jesus said, "Do not fear those who kill the body, but are unable to kill the soul; rather fear Him who is able to destroy both soul and body in hell" (Matthew 10:28). We must be more concerned about what God thinks than what men think. Even though we will be rejected by some and scorned and put down by others, we must not be concerned with whether or not the unbeliever will reject us. Instead we must tell him that he will not be rejected by God because of his sin—if he repents of it.

2. *Fear Of Losing Reputation*. The way to deal with this is easy—give up your reputation! Jesus made Himself of no reputation. (See Philippians 2:7.) When He was shamefully nailed to the cross, He had no reputation to lose. Our identity must be based in Jesus, not on our reputation in the world, whatever that may be.

Too many Christians never experience victory in this area simply because they continue basing their identity on something other than the Lord. If our identity is found in being a rational, level-headed person, then we will be tempted not to be too radical in our witness for fear we will be thought of as a religious fanatic. The same is true of our reputation on the job, in school, with peers, and the like.

I once saw a T-shirt that said, "I'm a fool for Christ, whose fool are you?" While we shouldn't *try* to be foolish, we must remember that the gospel message we preach sounds like foolishness to the natural mind. (See 1 Corinthians 1:18.) We must settle once and for all where our identity and reputation lies. As Paul said, "God forbid that I should glory, save in the cross of our Lord Jesus Christ, by whom the world is crucified unto me, and I unto the world'' (Galatians 6:14, *KJV*).

3. Fear Of Physical Harm. I have talked with Christians from Muslim countries whose lives have literally become endangered simply because they are Christians. Jesus warned that a time would come when Christians would be killed by people who thought they were doing God a favor, a fact borne out thousands of times over throughout history.

Our fear of rejection and losing reputation seems trifling when compared to Christians in some parts of the world who literally fear for their lives every time they witness to someone or hold a Bible study. We in the western world need to learn a lesson from these Christians. The Bible nowhere says we are exempt from physical harm or death for preaching the gospel. As a matter of fact, it promises just the opposite: "All who desire to live godly in Christ Jesus will be persecuted" (2 Timothy 3:12).

We must ask God for the faith and strength to stand firm in the face of any and every fear that Satan may throw at us, be it physical, mental, emotional, or spiritual. Remember Paul's words,

> I have been crucified with Christ; and it is no longer I who live, but Christ lives in me; and the life which I now live in the flesh I live by faith in the Son of God, who loved me, and delivered Himself up for me—Galatians 2:20.

4. Fear Of Being Inadequate. Here we feel we don't know enough to answer all the questions an unbeliever may ask of us, and some do ask difficult questions. Some who ask questions are just looking for an argument, while others, often spiritually hungry, are looking for earnest answers. We need to be sensitive to this so we don't become embroiled in arguments with people who are just wasting our time or neglect to give honest answers to those who *are* spiritually hungry. After all, they are the people who deserve honest answers to their questions, and we must be prepared to give them.

As we grow daily in our knowledge of God, we are never going to have all the answers to all the questions asked of us. When we don't know the answer to a question, we must be prepared to do some homework and search it out. Afterwards, we can arrange to meet with the person who asked the question and discuss the answer.

Researching in this way has a triple benefit. First, it shows the person we care about them and their question. Second, by their willingness to meet and discuss at a later time, we can measure their sincerity in asking the question. Finally, we grow in our knowledge and ability to answer the same question should someone else ask it in the future. We are exhorted by Peter to always be "ready to make a defense to everyone who asks you to give an account for the hope that is in you, yet with gentleness and reverence" (1 Peter 3:15).

One thing always to keep in mind is that even when we don't know the answer to a difficult question a non-Christian may ask, we do know Jesus and can testify to what He's done in our lives. The woman at the well is an example of this. Barely one day old in her faith, she testified and led many of her fellow Samaritans to Christ. (See John 4:39.)

Many other fears could be listed and expounded upon here, but most fall into one of the four categories we have discussed. When we experience any type of fear in evangelism, we must deal with it; otherwise it will cripple our witness for Jesus. We must not allow Satan to put us under condemnation because of our fears. If that happens, we will never see any hope for getting out from under them. Instead, we must be honest with God and ourselves about our fears.

We can learn a lesson from the early church, whose prayer in the midst of great suffering and persecution was,

> "And now, Lord, take note of their threats, and grant that Thy bond-servants may speak Thy word with all confidence . . . " And when they had prayed . . . they were all filled with the Holy Spirit, and began to speak the word of God with boldness—Acts 4:29-31.

We should not be discouraged if we never totally conquer all of these fears, but as we submit to Jesus and love Him we will begin to experience a substantial amount of victory over them. As we trust in God's character and continually place our trust in Him, our faith will be the victory that overcomes anything the world can throw at us, *including* the fear of man. (See 1 John 5:4-5.)

Note David's encouraging formula for victory over fear:

> God is our refuge and our strength, a very pleasant help in trouble. *Therefore we will not fear,* though the earth should change, and though the mountains slip into the heart of the sea—Psalm 46:1-2, *italics added.*

Having The Right Attitude

Most unbelievers are not stupid or ignorant and will often pick up a bad attitude in a person witnessing to them.

Self-righteousness, hypocrisy, pride and many other bad attitudes are easily spotted by non-Christians. In evangelism our attitude must be the foundation for our actions.

> Have this attitude in yourselves which was also in Christ Jesus, who, although He existed in the form of God, did not regard equality with God a thing to be grasped, but emptied Himself, taking the form of a bond-servant, and being made in the likeness of men—Philippians 2:5-7.

> If the foundations are destroyed, what can the righteous do?—Psalm 11:3.

Often we are ineffective in communicating the gospel, not because we don't say the right things, but because we say the right things with the wrong attitude. Speech teachers tell us that *how* you say something will get more response than the actual content of what you say.

1. *Don't Be Self-Righteous.* Evangelism has been described as one beggar telling another where he can find bread. Remember, we are only made righteous in Jesus Christ—not by our works—no matter how sanctified we think ourselves to be.

> By His doing you are in Christ Jesus, who became to us wisdom from God, and righteousness and sanctification, and redemption, that, just as it is written, "Let him who boasts, boast in the Lord"—1 Corinthians 1:30-31.

The very reason most people are lost is because most people are self-righteous. When we allow ourselves to come across in this manner, we are presenting the gospel in a wrong spirit. We must lift up Jesus as the author and finisher of our faith and let Him draw men to Himself.

2. *Don't Be Hypocritical.* We must live out what we profess to believe so that the name "Christian" becomes synonymous with a quality of living that truly reflects the character of Jesus. What we need is more biblical living, not more biblical talking. We must walk in holiness and trust in God's grace to overcome sin and hypocrisy in our lives.

3. *Don't Be Critical.* Several years ago I grew cold in my relationship with the Lord, and it showed itself in a lack of joy and faith, a growing legalism, and an absence of fruit in my evangelism. God revealed to me that I had developed a critical spirit and that my judging of others was having severe repercussions in every area of my Christian life. I repented of pride, the root of the problem, and, by the grace of God, was restored.

In the midst of this situation, God showed me a vision in which I was working on an assembly line. As long as I kept my eyes fixed on my work, everything went smoothly and the work got done. But when I began looking around at what others on the assembly line were doing, my work did not get done. This vision taught me a valuable lesson: To the extent that I spend my time criticizing and judging others, to that same extent my work, which God has specifically given me to do, will not get done. These words of Jesus need to be the rule by which we live: "I did not come to judge the world, but to save the world" (John 12:47).

While hanging on his twelve foot cross on Sunset Strip, Evangelist Arthur Blessitt led an acquaintance of mine to the Lord. Another friend got saved at a sex orgy when he forgot to turn off the television set that was airing a Billy Graham broadcast. One brother I know witnessed to a man in the stall next to him in a public restroom. He struck up a conversation about Jesus while they were both seated on their respective toilets and prayed with him right on the spot. They met each other face-to-face when they had each finished their business, and the follow-up began.

Other people have been converted at Christian rock concerts; in bars, churches, or coffee houses; on the street or the beach; at home; and in a myriad other such places. God will use any and every means possible, even things we may personally not agree with, to bring people to Himself. We must make sure we are doing exactly what He has called us to do rather than spending our time criticizing the means He has instructed others to use.

Having a clean spirit is essential to having an evangelistic lifestyle. Many evangelists may not do things the way we would like them to be done—that's okay; we need to be praying that God will bless their ministry. Paul rejoiced that the gospel was being preached, even when it was done out of a motive of envy or strife. (See Philippians 1:15-18.) Many unorthodox means of preaching the gospel have been used in the last two-thousand years, and many more will be tried in the future; but, as Paul said, do it by all means possible. (See 1 Corinthians 9:22.)

Don't allow a critical spirit to develop. Always keep these words in mind: "Let every man prove his own work, and then shall he have rejoicing in himself alone, and not in another" (Galatians 6:4, *KJV*). Likewise, John says, "Watch yourselves, that you might not lose what we have accomplished" (2 John 8).

4. *Don't See People As Statistics*. We shouldn't just be buttonholing non-believers with the attitude, "Just chalking up another soul for Christ." Instead we should be genuinely concerned for the welfare of the person to whom we are witnessing. The seemingly pious "God said it, so take it or leave it—turn or burn" posture many

Christians adopt in their witnessing is more effective in turning people off to the gospel than on to it. A caring relationship needs to grow with the person, as we love them with God's love. People don't really care how much we know until they know how much we care! Our love for the lost, not just in word but in action and deed, is the foundation upon which evangelism is built. (See 1 John 3:17-18.)

Horses And Mules

"Do not be as the horse or as the mule which have no understanding, whose trappings include bit and bridle to keep them in check" (Psalm 32:9).

The horse and the mule, I believe, represent two different types of Christians and how they approach witnessing. The horse represents the zealous, aggressive type of Christian whose zeal for evangelism calls to mind the image of a frisky thoroughbred waiting at the starting gate for the Kentucky Derby to begin. This type of Christian will witness to anyone and everyone, whether God tells them to or not. They don't like to beat around the bush but get straight to the point with the non-Christian. Their zeal and fire for God is commendable, but it needs to be tempered with a broken and contrite spirit. Otherwise their natural aggressiveness, which God gave them as a strength, can quickly turn to self-confidence, self-sufficiency, pride, and a critical spirit toward others who don't have the same "zeal."

The mule, by contrast, represents the soft-spoken, passive type of Christian. Whereas the horse will witness at the drop of a hat, the mule often needs visions, dreams, prophecies, angels singing, and bells ringing before he will "feel led" to share his faith. He needs a good kick in the hind parts to get moving into the harvest field for Jesus.

Horses and mules need each other in evangelism, and often the Lord will give us the opposite type to be our witnessing partner so we can be balanced. God wants to deliver us from both unrestrained zeal and apathetic indifference so we'll listen to His voice and be obedient as we go out to share the good news. We can learn a lesson from the example of a horse named Peter and a mule named Jonah; both learned their lessons the hard way.

Overcoming our fears and having the right attitudes alone does not make us a good evangelist, although they help. It is being sensitive to God's voice and witnessing when and where He tells us to—at work, home, our sports club, the streets, or any place sinners are—that makes us effective witnesses.

Just as in fishing, you fish where the fish are, so today's "fishers of men" must witness where the sinners are!

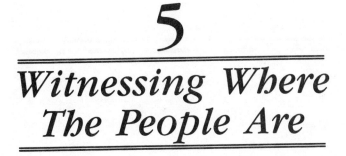

5

Witnessing Where The People Are

CHAPTER FIVE

Witnessing Where The People Are

Once I was witnessing outside a bar, and a man got very upset with me. Amidst a flurry of four-letter words, he told me the place for religion was in the church and that I should keep my message there. I told him I would like to, except for the fact that most sinners don't go to church!

Preaching is not for the church, and if we want to reach sinners, we must go where they are—on the street, in bars, their homes, on the job, and the like. Jesus told us to go into all the *world*—not the church—and preach the gospel. When challenged by the Pharisees as to why He ate and drank with tax collectors and sinners, Jesus replied, "I have not come to call the righteous but sinners to repentance" (Luke 5:32). The church is the place for *teaching* the Word of God, not preaching, so that those taught might be equipped to minister to a lost world—right where they are.

Witnessing Where You Are

Early in my walk with the Lord I had a desire to witness, but I didn't really know how. I kept asking the Lord for the right atmosphere, situation, and timing. Sometimes I found that witnessing flowed smoothly; at others it just didn't go right at all. And those "in season" opportunities for witnessing didn't seem to come often enough. Then I discovered Paul's exhortation to his young disciple Timothy to be ready in season and out: "Preach the word; be ready in season and out of season" (2 Timothy 4:2).

The Greek words for "in season and out of season" can be translated, *conveniently* and *inconveniently*. There are times when it is more convenient to witness than others, but just because it is inconvenient doesn't mean the Spirit does not want us to share. A good rule to follow is to presume God wants us to share the gospel with everyone unless He leads otherwise. After all, He has already told us to tell "every creature" and will prepare a way for us to do just that.

Since becoming a Christian, I've worked in a restaurant, a cannery, on a Christmas tree farm, as a construction laborer and cement finisher, and in "full-time" ministry. In each of these situations I have had many opportunities to be God's missionary to the people with whom I worked. Sometimes it was convenient to share; other times it was not. But His promise was always there to keep me going: "My word . . . shall not return to Me empty, without accomplishing what I desire" (Isaiah 55:11).

When I was about six months old in my relationship with the Lord, I worked at a spinach cannery. While I didn't know many Bible verses, I had a story to tell. I was rejected by many as I tried to share the good news with them, but some, like Lorraine, listened. She was a street-wise young woman who came to work every day with a switchblade in her pocket. Both Lorraine and her tough boyfriend named Louie rejected the Lord at first, and Louie even threatened to stab me. To make a long story short, I didn't get stabbed, Lorraine got saved, and Louie got fired! Today Lorraine sings in an Assembly of God choir.

Norman and I worked together on the cannery assembly line. He argued with me for weeks about the irrelevancy of the gospel and how he believed all roads led to God. But God got him before spinach season was over, and today he's a fire fighter for Christ!

Eileen worked further along the same assembly line and used to ask me questions about God and the Bible during our ten minute breaks. I couldn't answer many of her questions straight away and often had to do some homework. But Eileen eventually gave her life to Jesus as well.

Pat Brown threw the tract I gave her on the ground in disgust. Later, though, she accepted Jesus as her Lord and is actively involved in a full-gospel church today. At first, Janice covered her emptiness by rejecting my witness, but later I had the privilege of both leading her to Christ and baptizing her. She is now serving the Lord in Minnesota.

These are my spinach cannery stories, and they could be echoed thousands of times over by many other Christians in various jobs around the world who witness right where they are. Your job, family, neighborhood, etc. are ready-made situations in which God has placed you to be His witness. We don't need to wait for dreams, visions, ringing bells, or audible voices before we start sharing our faith. We are already called to abide in Christ and be active witnesses for Him wherever He has placed us. (See 1 Corinthians 7:24.)

Some people are mistakenly waiting to be sent to the mission field before they witness regularly and are missing out on many glorious opportunities to lead people to a relationship with Jesus Christ. Step out in faith and witness today—right where you are!

The Divine Appointment

As we continue to walk with the Lord, we grow in our ability to be sensitive to His leading in our life, both in day-to-day matters and when we are out sharing our faith with others. A good practice is to schedule a time into our weekly routine that we use specifically for sharing the good news about Jesus with the lost. We schedule and discipline every other area of our life—going to work, recreation, entertainment, Bible studies, prayer meetings, and so on. So why not schedule a weekly time to spend with non-Christians in whatever type of outreach or friendship evangelism that seems applicable?

Don't just wait passively for it to happen, but *passionately pursue* "divine appointments" that the Holy Spirit arranges in the course of your day. Often we are so engrossed in our daily affairs that divine appointments just seem like another interruption. We must be alert and actively seeking them.

On a recent plane trip, an elderly man sat next to me. I was physically tired and not really "in the mood" for witnessing, but before long I struck up a conversation with him. Soon he was pouring his heart out to me in regard to his health, having recently been diagnosed with terminal cancer and given only three months to live. I asked him about his relationship with God, and he admitted that his recent diagnosis had awakened a spiritual hunger within him. On that flight I had the privilege of leading him to Christ. It was a divine appointment, and even though I hadn't been looking for it, God had arranged it. After all, He's in control of my schedule!

Petrus, a young man from Micronesia, was waiting at a local street corner for the crossing light to change when Mike and I met him. I pulled a gospel tract out and began talking to him about his spiritual life, inviting him to a coffee house to continue the conversation. After about ten minutes he told us that just three days earlier he had asked God to reveal Himself. Now he marvelled at the "coincidence" of meeting Mike and me.

Several other coincidences also just seemed to line up. His brother's house (where he was staying), for instance, stood right across the street from the church I would be preaching at that Sunday—which was also close to where I lived so I could continue seeing him. Petrus went back to Micronesia a changed man—all because of a divine appointment.

Early in 1986, a young couple from Gospel Outreach church in Springfield, Oregon, were having a mediocre day of door-to-door evangelism. Shortly before they decided to stop for the day, they were invited into the house of a young lady who seemed open to the gospel. On a subsequent visit, they were able to lead her to the Lord. She later explained that at the very moment they knocked on her door on their first visit she had a pistol to her head and was trying to muster the courage to pull the trigger. By divine appointment, two willing workers were able to help her find eternal life instead of a bullet in the head!

Goutam was a young radical from the communist governed state of West Bengal, India. While on a train from Calcutta to his home town of Uluberia, he "just happened" to sit next to two *Youth With A Mission* workers who diligently shared the gospel with him. Over the next few days following the encounter, Goutam began to see the emptiness of his communist ideology and came to believe that Jesus was the answer to the emptiness he was feeling. He turned his life over to God and became a radical for Jesus Christ. Today Goutam is involved in church planting in northern India. He attributes his conversion to the "perfectly timed" divine appointment on a train bound for glory!

Recently I was driving in my car listening to Dr. James Dobson's *Focus on the Family* radio show. He recommended a book for children's Bible bedtime stories, and I immediately turned the car around to go to the bookstore. On my way into the store, the secretary at the radio station (which was next door) asked me to come in and take a phone call from a listener who was asking questions that she couldn't answer. I talked to a man named Charley who, after his questions were answered, was ready to accept the Lord. I had the privilege of leading him to Christ over the phone.

I was traveling in and out of town right after the encounter and was therefore frustrated in my follow-up attempts. After a month, I was finally able to visit Charley and found that he had been sovereignly led to some members of a full-gospel church, who followed him up and baptized him. In a seemingly normal course of events, I can now look back and see God's sovereign hand guiding my steps into a divine appointment to lead a soul to Christ.

Divine appointments sometimes come as the result of random encounters—and when we least expect them. At other times we will feel a spiritual inclination to approach someone with a question—maybe a word of wisdom or knowledge that God has given us for them. Regardless of how an encounter happens, we need to be expecting the unexpected. Then we will begin to see those "interruptions" that beset us in the course of our day as ordained of God to bring someone into His Kingdom. In this way, every day becomes an adventure as God begins to arrange our circumstances for His glory!

The Witnessing Dialogue

In personal evangelism, it is important that we don't seek so much to preach *at* people, as to talk *to* them about a relationship with Jesus Christ. Talking implies that we have dialogue with a person, and in dialogue listening is just as important as speaking. We must learn to listen as well as talk in our conversations with people about the Lord.

> The Lord has given Me the tongue of disciples, that I may know how to sustain the weary one with a word. He awakens Me morning by morning, He awakens My ear to listen as a disciple—Isaiah 50:4.

Jesus' method of evangelism usually centered around asking questions, listening to the reply, and responding to it with the words of life. By listening, He understood that the woman of Samaria needed living water and that Nicodemas needed to hear about being born again. He was able to respond to their area of need *because He listened*.

Often we will not discover a person's area of need until we start asking them questions and sensitively listen to their answers. This requires discipline, for our tendency is to be thinking of the next thing we are going to say while the other person is talking. We know that everyone needs to be saved, but the real issue is, how do we most effectively present Christ in a particular situation? After all, we are not selling salvation-in-a-can but are presenting a *personal* Lord and Savior who is able to meet the individual's need. We can do this effectively by truly listening and hearing what they are saying while at the same time expecting them to listen patiently as we respond to what they have said.

While I was witnessing on Union Square in San Francisco, a young man started telling me all the reasons why he could not be saved, going on and on with the standard excuses—too many hypocrites, the Bible is a myth, what about all the pygmies in Africa, and so on. After listening for about twenty minutes, I began wondering if I was just wasting time. Then I heard the Holy Spirit whisper to me, "Just hear him out."

After another forty-five minutes of ramblings, he went off to buy some cigarettes, inviting me to go with him to the bar for a drink. When I accepted his invitation, he seemed a little shocked; but while I sipped my coke, he began pouring his heart out, telling me about the hurts and fears that had plagued him all his life. He literally cried in his beer as I shared the gospel with him, urging him to give his life to the Lord. He didn't, but he left that bar promising me he would give serious consideration to receiving Jesus.

Sometimes we need to *earn* the right to speak to a person by giving them a hearing ear. This takes time, but if we really love people as Jesus did, we will take that time—sinners are worth it!

Interest Doors

Using an interest door simply means taking advantage of a common interest you may have with an unbeliever through which you can share the gospel. Jesus, for example, used water as an interest door to show the woman at the well her need for living water. (See John 4.)

In fact, much of Jesus' teaching and preaching revolved around the use of interest doors. He didn't use abstract theological terms in communicating truth but spoke of everyday life situations and gave them spiritual relevance.

He spoke of fishing, farming, giving birth, baking bread, tending sheep, opening doors, selling pearls, finding treasures, tasting salt, etc. He told stories, asked questions, gave comparisons, and used illustrations to drive home the truths He wanted to convey.

We could learn a lesson from Jesus and bring the gospel "down to earth" rather than get involved in speaking the "Christianese" language—"Have you been washed in the blood?" "Have you crucified your old man yet?" "Are you redeemed?" "You need to get committed!" "You need to find a good body." Without an interpreter, oftentimes the non-Christian can draw some obvious wrong conclusions from what you are saying.

Paul used the altar to the Unknown God and some Greek poetry as an interest door through which to share the gospel with the philosophers of Mars Hill. (See Acts 17:22-31.)

An interest door allows the Holy Spirit to take an everyday topic and use it as an opportunity to share the gospel message. For instance, in 1983 there was a TV movie called *The Day After* that depicted the aftermath of a nuclear war. It was soon the topic of everyone's conversation. The film ended with two men, totally without hope, crying on each others shoulders. This scene, which left the eighty million Americans who watched it with the same hopeless feeling, provided an interest door through which to share the hope that is in Christ. Many Christians took advantage of it.

We need to be informed as to what is happening in our world. Local and world news, politics, economics, entertainment, and even sports are all effective interest doors. As we share, we also need to be praying that our topical approach will spark interest in an unbeliever's heart so that we can go on and present the gospel to them.

After teaching at a church in California one afternoon, I picked up a hitchhiker as I drove through town. Noticing that he had the logo of the rock group Black Sabbath (a group known for its satanic overtones) on the front of his cap, I asked him if he liked the group. He responded, "Yeah."

"Aren't they into the devil?" I went on.

"That's what I heard," he replied. So I asked him if he was into the devil. He told me he wasn't—he just liked the group's music.

"Well, I'm into God!" I told him and spent about twenty minutes sitting in the car in front of his house, talking with him and giving my testimony. He opened up and began to tell me some deep needs he had in his life. He had just been sentenced to four months in jail for some crimes he had committed, and so I was able to arrange for members of the church to follow-up on him. Soon they were busy studying the Bible with him in the jail. It started with the good work of giving him a ride. (See Matthew 5:16.) Then, using his love of rock music as an interest door, I was able to share the gospel.

Once I was asked to be a guest speaker at some outreach meetings that several churches were holding in a tent at a local park in California. I was preparing for one of my messages when I felt distinctly impressed by the Lord to include an illustration from Peter Stoner's book, *Science Speaks*. The illustration had to do with the statistical probability of one man fulfilling the Old Testament prophecies relating to the Messiah. (Stoner had calculated the odds of one individual fulfilling just eight prophecies as equivalent to covering the entire state of Texas two feet deep in silver dollars and then asking a blindfolded man to pull out one specially marked coin on his first try. Jesus actually fulfilled over 300 prophecies, which, of course, raises the odds to almost unbelievable!)

Jim, a student at a local junior college, attended the service in which I shared the illustration. At the end of the service I gave an invitation for those present to receive Christ, and Jim responded.

Six months later I met Jim at a church, and he shared his story with me. "I wasn't necessarily interested in spiritual things, but I had some free time that night. So I went to the tent meeting. I happened to be studying the science of compound probability in one of my classes at the time, so your illustration about the prophecies awakened my interest enough to consider seriously who Jesus claimed to be. By the time you reached the altar call, I had made my decision."

Jim had responded to the gospel because it was shared through an interest door that was relevant, personal, and applicable to him at the time. I believe I received a "Word in Season" about what Jim needed to hear. (See Isaiah 50:4.) God is faithful to give us the wisdom that it takes to win souls. At times, as in Jim's case, God gives a preacher a "word" in a message for the congregation that is especially aimed at an individual.

Out On The Streets

That our sons may be as plants grown up in their youth; that our daughters may be as corner stones, polished after the similitude of a palace: that our garners may be full, affording all manner of store: that our sheep may bring forth thousands and ten thousands in our streets—Psalm 144:12-13.

Youth With A Mission runs a street ministry on Hotel Street in the red-light district of Honolulu. Once I was witnessing to one of the regular patrons, and he asked me why church people would be in such an apparently God-forsaken place as Hotel Street. Without thinking, I replied, "You know, if Jesus were to come to town, this is probably the first place He would visit."

As I reflected on this statement, I realized the truth of it. Jesus didn't come to call the righteous but sinners to repentance. (See Luke 5:32.) Hotel Street is as high on His priority list as any other street. I believe God can use us to bring many souls into His Kingdom right on the street. After all, Jesus and the apostles took their message to the streets, and He has told us to go into the streets and alleys of the city and compel people to come to Him. (See Luke 14:23.)

One of the things I enjoy about cities is the multitude of people whom I can talk to about Jesus. As I witness to a person on the street and find my message rejected, immediately I can go to another and another—until I find someone who wants to hear about Jesus. If you have never witnessed on the streets before, team up with someone who has experience at it and get your feet wet—you'll be glad you did!

Street Witnessing—The Approach

Just how do I approach a total stranger on the street and start talking to him about Jesus? This is the dilemma many Christians find themselves in when beginning street witnessing. To be honest, I haven't found many suave, debonair ways of breaking into conversation about Jesus with a person on the street. Remember, most people aren't on the street just waiting for someone to come up and tell them about Jesus, so there is bound to be a little awkwardness no matter how good our approach gets.

The first thing we must do is believe God has prepared the way before us. Psalm 37:23 says, "The steps of a man are established by the Lord." Believe that even the rejections we encounter will be used by God to spur us on to a fruitful witnessing experience. Be looking for divine appointments, and ask God to show you the right interest door through which to share the gospel. The interest door approach will make the transition from the natural to the spiritual easier.

Recently in Waikiki, I noticed a sidewalk vendor selling pearls in the oyster to passing tourists. Walking over to him, I asked, "Have you ever heard of the pearl of great price?" Astonished, he looked at me and told me he hadn't, so I used the opening to share Jesus' story of the pearl merchant with him. I went on to tell him all I knew the Bible had to say on pearls—the pearly gates, don't cast your pearls before swine, and so forth.

When I could see he was tiring of hearing about biblical pearls, I asked him to share about pearls in the oyster with me. He did, and before long the conversation was back around to the gospel. We talked for another forty-five minutes or so, and it all started through a pearly interest door!

People on the street are often in a hurry, so I have found that being direct is a good approach. Don't be afraid to be honest; state why you are there, and trust that God has prepared the way before you. Often I use a gospel tract, approaching a person with a smile and saying, "Could I just give you this to read?" or, "Would you like some good news?" even, "Did you know Jesus loves you?"

Sometimes I don't even use a tract but just approach someone and ask for a few minutes of their time to share something important to them. There is a great advantage in being this direct: If a person doesn't want to hear what you have to say, they can tell you right at the outset. Then you can find someone who *does* want to hear instead of wasting each other's time.

Organizations like *Campus Crusade, Evangelism Explosion, Christian Equippers,* and others have used various surveys and questionnaires as a way of breaking into conversation. Questions such as, "If you were to die tonight, do you have the assurance you would go to heaven?" and, "Who in your opinion was Jesus Christ?" have been used as effective means to open up fruitful conversations about Christ. Remember, in witnessing you must be comfortable with the approach you choose.

Street Preaching

When I first became a Christian, street preaching was last on my list of priorities in serving God. The stereotype of a "gloom and doom" hell-fire preacher, scowl on his face, holding a sandwich board, and wearing sackcloth and ashes while screaming at people to repent was not something I wanted to be a part of. It wasn't that I had anything against preaching, but most street preachers I had ever seen looked as though they had come from another planet!

As I began to study Scripture, though, I noticed that open-air preaching was often mentioned. Soon I began to realize that it had a valid place in today's world. "What I tell you in the darkness, speak in the light; and what you hear whispered in your ear, proclaim upon the housetops" (Matthew 10:27). It was then that the Lord spoke to my heart, "Okay, Danny, since you think street preachers are weird, *you* go and preach on the streets—only don't be weird!"

There are times when street preaching is not appropriate, and we must be sensitive to the Lord while at the same time using common sense. In my own evangelism on the streets, I have found that one-on-one dialogue is the most fruitful. But crowded streets, parks, and squares, especially in the city, are conducive to open-air rallies and house-top type preaching. In such places large numbers of people can be reached in a short amount of time.

Music, street drama, and mime often help in drawing a crowd before the gospel is preached. Groups such as *Open Air Campaigners* have incorporated sketchboard sermons, rope tricks, and flash-cards into their presentation of the gospel.

While some object to the use of such gimmicks, we must remember that, when we are on the streets, we need to be creative. People just aren't walking around on the streets with hymnals in hand waiting for church to start! The issue in any method of evangelism is communication. Are we communicating the gospel effectively? Methods that worked twenty years ago may not work today, and methods that work in Bangkok may not work in Chicago. We must be creative, flexible, and open to the guidance of the Lord of the Harvest.

Literature Evangelism

Modern Christians have yet to realize the full value of the printed page. With little money and only a handful of committed workers, we can saturate large populations with gospel literature. Scores of people have come to know the Lord through gospel books and tracts.

My first real exposure to Jesus Christ came in 1972 on a California beach. Someone handed me a copy of the

Hollywood Free Paper, a gospel tabloid published during the Jesus movement that contained testimonies of champion surfers who had recently become Christians. These spoke to my heart, and it wasn't long afterwards that my life was radically changed.

Throughout history, Christians have made valuable use of the printed page. John Wesley founded Britain's first tract society, while Luther, Calvin, and other reformers reached millions through their tracts. William Carey shook the evangelical world of his day with the widely publicized tract, "An Inquiry into the Obligation of Christians to use Means for the Conversion of the Heathen." George Verwer, founder of *Operation Mobilization*, was converted after someone sent him the Gospel of John in the mail.

Today, groups such as *Last Days Ministries, The American Tract Society*, and *Good News Underground* offer tracts and materials free of charge. We would do well to take advantage of all that these paper missionaries have to offer us. It was Karl Marx who remarked that the short pamphlet is the most powerful of all revolutionary tools; and, according to Mahatma Ghandi's nephew, in India, "The missionaries taught us to read, but the communists gave us the literature." Such a comment should stir us to fill the world with gospel literature.

Literature evangelism, like mass evangelism and street preaching, has some inherent weaknesses. For example, it is not as personal as a conversation, and a gospel tract can't disciple anyone. But passing out tracts on the street or distributing them to people we meet in the course of our day can be a stepping-stone to developing boldness in witnessing. When starting out, it is easier to pass out gospel literature rather than going straight into a witnessing conversation. Remember, literature has the power to speak to a person's heart and open up a door to share more later through conversation.

I have found writing my own gospel tracts to be effective. When I first got involved in literature evangelism, I often felt uncomfortable with the particular tracts that were available. I was never comfortable with the "Frankenstein" type—the kind with a cover cartoon of a person screaming out in agony from the flames of hell. I felt I could avoid this type of excess by writing my own tracts. (See Appendix B.) In general, I have found people more receptive if I am giving them something that *I* have written. There is also something more personal about handing out my own tract; it is an expression of my heart on paper.

You may like to consider writing your own tract and having it printed. You can have a thousand copies typeset and printed for less than a hundred dollars. Keep it short and to the point. If no ideas seem particularly appropriate, then write down your testimony, put your picture on the front of it, passport style (but smiling), and call it, "My Story," or something similar. Be sure to include your name and phone number on the back so people can contact you personally if they want to know more. Be creative, but, remember, keep it simple.

Christian books are another excellent tool to use in literature evangelism, and countless numbers of people have been converted through reading them. Chuck Colson describes leaning on the steering wheel of his car and crying like a baby after reading *Mere Christianity* by C.S. Lewis. Through the book, the Holy Spirit had been able to pinpoint the sin of pride in his heart, and soon afterwards he surrendered his life to Christ.

Many contemporary books, such as, *More Than A Carpenter* by Josh McDowell, *The Late Great Planet Earth* by

Hal Lindsey, and *Joni* by Joni Eareckson Tada, have all been used to draw people to the Lord.

Door-To-Door Evangelism

> I did not shrink from declaring to you anything that was profitable, and teaching you publicly and from house to house, solemnly testifying to both Jews and Greeks of repentance toward God and faith in our Lord Jesus Christ—Acts 20:20-21.

Recently, a girl from one of our *YWAM* door-to-door witnessing teams came to me rather distressed after an afternoon of house-to-house visitation. She had spent two and a half hours with a Filipino family who had become Jehovah's Witnesses. Knowing that Filipinos are predominantly Catholic, I asked how it was that this family had joined the Watchtower. I could have put the words in her mouth before she answered. They had been faithfully attending the Catholic church they were raised in until about three years ago when two Jehovah's Witnesses knocked on their door. The two were very persuasive and promptly seduced the family into joining one of the nation's largest cults!

I used to look on door-to-door evangelism with disdain since Jehovah's Witnesses, Mormons, and other cults all engaged in it. But, although I did not want to be linked with them, I started to see that I was playing right into the devil's hand. All over the world, thousands of unsuspecting people are being deceived and led astray right in their own living rooms. This should provoke us to get to the door *before* the cults. Today, many who are in the Jehovah's

Witnesses and the Mormon Church could very well have been won to the Body of Christ had we gotten to their door first.

The cults go door-to-door trying to earn their salvation by doing good works. How much more should we, who have salvation by grace, offer this grace with *at least* the same zeal that the cults display. Jesus said, "I have come to cast fire on the earth; how I wish that it were already kindled" (Luke 12:49).

Listed below are some guidelines to remember when engaging in door-to-door evangelism:

1. Go out in pairs, ideally a man and a woman or husband and wife team.

2. Be respectful. Remember, you are on someone's private property. Don't walk on the lawn, hop the fence, or snoop around the house before knocking on the door.

3. Once you have knocked or rung the door-bell, take a step backwards so you don't appear pushy. If no one is at home, leave some gospel literature—with a contact number—in the door. (Don't put it in the mailbox; it's illegal to do so in some countries.)

4. Smile, be pleasant and relaxed, and introduce yourself. Tell the person who answers the door where you are from (First Baptist, *YWAM*, neighborhood Bible study, etc.) and why you are there. As in street witnessing, some have used surveys and questionnaires as conversation openers. If you feel comfortable with this, go for it! If not, ask if you can have a few minutes of their time to share the gospel. It's at this introductory stage that we often get the most nervous.

Bruce and Lucy, for example, were going door-to-door in Sydney, Australia. Bruce was so nervous that when he introduced himself at the door he said, "Hi, *I'm Lucy and this is Bruce,* and we'd like to share the good news of Jesus with you!" The man at the door laughed and decided that if they were willing to go witnessing being that nervous, then they must have something worth listening to. He invited them in and later invited Jesus into his life.

5. If you are invited in, accept the hospitality graciously. It is often good to compliment them on something in their house—a picture, furniture, or something of that nature—since this helps break the ice and relax both parties. Ask questions and develop a dialogue that will get the person thinking about their relationship with God.

If the TV is on, politely ask if they can turn it down a little (most often they will shut it off). If they have small children, one of you could entertain them in another part of the room so they won't be a distraction. Be careful not to take them out of sight or the parent may worry about their safety with a stranger.

If a person becomes uncomfortable during the course of the conversation, you should excuse yourself politely—unless you discern their discomfort is the result of the conviction of sin. Thank them for their time and ask if they would be interested in further dialogue. If so, arrange a specific time at *their convenience* in the near future. If they are not interested, leave some good gospel literature and a contact phone number, preferably your own. Remember also, you only asked for a few moments of their time—don't wear out your welcome!

6. If you are not invited into the house, politely ask if there is a more convenient time for you to stop by. If there isn't, try and leave some good gospel literature. Remember, always be respectful, polite, and loving.

7. Be organized. Keep good records so you can efficiently follow-up and go back to contact those who were not home.

There are many methods for sharing the gospel. Our God is creative, and we are "partakers of [His] divine nature" (2 Peter 1:4). We share His creativity. While many ways could be discussed in this chapter, I will limit them to two major areas: music and drama.

Gospel Music

William Booth, founder of the Salvation Army, used to put Christian lyrics to the popular pub tunes of his day. His Hallelujah Lassies would sing them on the streets to share the gospel. This led to accusations of worldliness, but Booth's simple defense was, "Why should the devil have all the good tunes?" Throughout history, from King David to Keith Green, contemporary music has been used to express God's heart of compassion.

Without getting into a debate on rock music, let me say that, in order to communicate, music must be accepted and appreciated by the ears that hear it. Parents often accuse their children of not being able to appreciate good music but fail to realize that the definition of "good" music changes from generation to generation. The issue to consider when evaluating gospel music is not whether the beat is syncopated or how loud it is but, rather, is it anointed and is it communicating the gospel? Have people been saved, blessed, and brought closer to Jesus as a result of a particular type of contemporary gospel music? If they have, then use it for the glory of God! (See 1 Thessalonians 5:21.)

Jesus said, "I did not come to judge the world, but to save the world" (John 12:47). That should be our motto. I have seen Christian rock bands win hundreds to Christ, and we must continually utilize the kind of music that will relate to contemporary people in today's society if we want to see many brought into the Kingdom of God.

Many letters have appeared in *Last Days Magazine* from people who have been saved after listening to a Keith Green album or tape, and many children have heard the gospel through the music from "Agapeland." Be sensitive with the use of music in evangelism, and be on the lookout for Christian concerts to which you can take a non-Christian friend or contemporary albums you can give them.

Gospel Drama

Gospel drama can range from puppets in child evangelism or skits on the street to full-fledged gospel musical productions, such as Jimmy and Carol Owens' *The Witness*. Throughout the Bible, God uses visual aids to help get His point across to His people. From Isaiah's going naked and Hosea's marrying a harlot to Jeremiah at the potter's house, God has done everything in His power to illustrate His message and help us *see* the gospel more clearly. We need to keep in mind that the gospel can be *seen* as well as heard. (See Romans 15:21.) Jesus' parables were only pictures He drew in the minds of His hearers to help them understand the Kingdom of God a little more clearly.

YWAM's allegorical dramas, *Toymaker and Son* and *Tribute*, have been used to reach many thousands around the world. Trained teams have performed them in back alleys and prisons and at official receptions in nearly every nation on earth. Others, such as Mike Warnke and Isaac Air Freight, have used comedy to present the truth of the gospel message, while Andre Cole uses "Gospel Magic" as an interest door to reach young people.

By its very nature, the potential of creativity is almost endless, and in the place of prayer we must allow the Holy Spirit to flood our minds and imaginations with ideas to use in effectively presenting the gospel.

The methods of evangelism discussed in this chapter are not just for the so-called "evangelists" in the church. No, they are for all Christians to be involved in, each doing their part as a worker in God's harvest field.

6

Workers For The Harvest

CHAPTER SIX

Workers For The Harvest

Several years ago I led a young man, Randy, to the Lord and brought him home to live in our community and be discipled. For more than a month we poured ourselves into him, teaching him the Bible and the ways of God, and it seemed he was making good progress. Then one morning we awoke to find that Randy had left and, in the process, stolen our complete sound system!

I was discouraged greatly by Randy's departure. Although he wasn't the first of our converts to backslide, he was the one who most surprised us. Feeling that I was somehow responsible for Randy's lapse in faith, I soon wanted to give up. It seemed that so much of my labor had been in vain.

In the midst of this turmoil, as I poured my heart out to God one day, I heard the voice of the Spirit whisper to my heart, "Danny, do you take the credit when you are able to lead someone to Me?" "No, Lord, You get all the glory from that," I quickly responded. "All right, then, don't take the blame when they backslide or reject the gospel," was the Lord's reply.

After this I discovered the following parable from Mark's gospel and began to meditate on it.

> So is the kingdom of God, as if a man should cast seed into the ground; and should sleep, and rise night and day, and the seed should spring and grow up, he knoweth not how. For the earth bringeth forth fruit of herself; first the blade, then the ear, after that the full corn in the ear. But when the fruit is brought forth, immediately he putteth in the sickle, because the harvest is come—Mark 4:26-29.

Soon I began to feel a tremendous burden lift off of my shoulders. I still felt bad about Randy's backsliding, and I continued to pray for his restoration; but I no longer blamed myself for what had happened. I had done everything I could to see him firmly grounded in the gospel, and he had chosen to reject it. It wasn't God's fault, and it wasn't my fault—it was Randy's choice.

My job is neither to save people nor keep them saved. I learned from the seed-planter parable that, in the harvest field, there is certain work that I must do, and there is other work that only God can do. My responsibility is to plow, plant, water, and harvest the fruit when it is ripe. It is God's responsibility to ensure that the seed grows.

In the parable, the man planted the seed and then went to bed. While he slept the seed grew, and, we are told, he did not know how this occurred. (See verse 27.) The reason for this was because he could not personally cause the seed to grow, it was *beyond his control*. Only God can do that; it is His work.

Jesus said, "No one can come to Me, unless the Father who sent Me draws him" (John 6:44). It is the Father who causes the seed to grow until it becomes "full corn" and ready for harvest.

The same principle is given in Paul's letter to the Corinthians:

> I planted, Apollos watered, but God was causing the growth. So then neither the one who plants nor the one who waters is anything, but God who causes the growth. . . . For we are God's fellow workers—1 Corinthians 3:6-9.

Conversion—A Process

In the parable of the seed-planter, Jesus teaches us about the process a person goes through in coming to Him for salvation. The sickle harvesting the fruit represents a person being converted to Christ, while the seed being planted and growing to the blade, ear, and full corn stages represents the spiritual growth a person goes through even before salvation.

Seed in Jesus' parables most often refers to the Word of God, so the full corn in the plant represents that Word doing its complete regenerating work. Jesus spoke of this as being born again. After conception, there is still nine months of "gestational" growth before the baby is actually born. If it is removed earlier than this, most likely it will not survive. Likewise, if corn is harvested too early, then the fruit will not be mature or longlasting.

In both of these illustrations, we see the salvation experience as a process that takes time—gestation. Some conversions happen instantly, but in the vast majority of cases people come to the Lord over a period of time. During this time, the Lord of the Harvest uses a variety of different workers and situations to deal with a person's heart and draw them to Himself. Few Christians would tell you they were converted the very first instance they heard the gospel; it took time.

Pray For Workers

Knowing the inner dynamics of conversion and the time it takes for a person to come to salvation, Jesus exhorted us to pray for laborers who could be sent into the harvest field. (See Matthew 9:37-38 and Luke 10:2.) He didn't ask us to pray for harvesters, sowers, plowers, or waterers exclusively but for workers—someone willing to do whatever is needed to bring the seed to harvest.

I believe every unbeliever in the world today is at a particular stage of growth in their relationship to God. Perhaps they have heard the Word but wouldn't allow it (ie. the seed) to take root and grow in their life. Maybe they heard and believed, but not enough to repent and commit their life to Christ (the blade). Possibly they are on the verge of salvation and just need a little more watering (the ear) or are ripe and ready to be harvested (full corn in the ear).

This is not intended to be taken to the letter, since not all unbelievers go exactly through all four stages of growth. But it does illustrate the fact that we must allow room for the Word of God to mature in a person's heart *before* they are harvested.

As workers in God's harvest field, our task is to discern a person's point of spiritual growth and what work needs to be done to bring them to the mature harvestable state. In our evangelistic mission, we must see ourselves as workers with different pieces of equipment clipped to our spiritual belts, ready to use as the need arises.

Perhaps, for instance, an unbeliever is hard-hearted and refuses to listen to the gospel. I might just try to love him and be his friend, letting my light shine by doing a good work for him. By using the hand trowel on my belt to break up the hard ground of his heart, I can then pray that the Lord of the Harvest will send another worker along who can nurture what has begun. (See Matthew 9:37-38 and Luke 10:2.)

If, on the other hand, a person has never heard the gospel but is willing to listen, I reach to the other side of my belt and pull some seed from my seed-bag. With it, I sow God's Word in that person's heart. If a person has been witnessed to and I sense all he needs is encouragement to come to salvation, I may unclip my watering can and water the seed that has already been sown.

Perhaps the person is ripe, mature, and ready for harvesting. Then I get out my sickle and "harvest," leading them in a prayer of commitment to Jesus. While I always try to bring the people I meet to salvation, I have to remind myself continually that it is the Lord who gives the increase. That often takes time, depending on the unbeliever's level of growth. I know of no greater joy than seeing the seed we plant in a person's life grow and be harvested.

God Gives The Increase

Hitchhiking home one day after a time of street witnessing, I was picked up by a guy named Gene. I had forgotten about it, until I met Gene in a department store ten years later. As we talked, he was happy to report to me that he, his wife, and his family had recently received Christ and been baptized. He went on to thank me for the Bible I had given him as I climbed out of his car; it had planted the seed in his life, and he and his wife were still reading it. God had given the increase.

Back in my hometown recently, I passed a young man on the street who looked familiar to me, so I stopped and asked him if he knew where we had met. At first he couldn't recall, but then, suddenly, he said, "Now I remember. Five years ago I was a street person living under a local bridge. One day you saw me sitting on the street with my backpack, approached me, and gave me a little red gospel booklet that told about Jesus. I used to read that little booklet every day. Within six months of that I was born again. Now I am involved with a Catholic Charismatic church." This young man went on to thank me for the seed I had planted in his heart.

After talking to hundreds of Christians about their conversion experience, I have found that in nearly every case a period of time passed from their first exposure to the gospel until their conversion. This time factor ranged from just a few hours to forty years or more. One writer documents a survey taken among active church members revealing that they had been exposed to an average of 5.76 different Christian influences prior to their conversion. Drop-outs, by comparison, had seen or heard the Christian message only 2.16 times before their decision.[1] This should make clear the need for more workers in the field to sow, water, and reap.

Why some people take much longer than others on their route to salvation remains a mystery, but there are several factors to consider. First, tremendous spiritual warfare is centered around a person's salvation. The Bible tells us that all unbelievers are blinded to the truth by the "god of this world'' (2 Corinthians 4:4). It often takes time to preach and pray these blinders off a person's spiritual eyes so that they can see the "light of the knowledge of the glory of God in the face of Christ" (2 Corinthians 4:6).

Second, even after the blinders have been removed, the unbeliever still has a free will and can choose to resist and reject the gospel or open up and accept it. If they reject the gospel, then we need to pray and ask God to deal more severely with them. God will not force a person into salvation against their will, but He will put the pressure on!

Saul of Tarsus, for example, was knocked to the ground, heard the audible voice of Jesus from heaven, and was blinded for three days before he was healed and filled with the Holy Spirit. God did not exactly force Saul's will, but He made the man an offer that was hard to refuse. (See Acts 9.) God has His way of getting the attention of a selfish heart set on doing its own thing, and intercession becomes an important part of evangelism since it releases the hand of God to deal in a person's life.

Other considerations in relation to the time factor of salvation are the degree of the power of God upon us as we witness, our unity in the church, and our example as believers to an unbelieving world.

When sharing the gospel, we must never forget that *God wants that person to be saved more than we do.* We must not think for a moment that He is not willing or able to save anyone and everyone. The Bible contains many explicit verses that declare God's feelings toward unbelievers. Consider the following Scripture verses:

> [God] desires all men to be saved and to come
> to the knowledge of the truth—1 Timothy 2:4.

> The Lord is . . . not willing that any should perish but that all should come to repentance—2 Peter 3:9, *KJV.*

> "As I live!" declares the Lord God, "I take no pleasure in the death of the wicked, but rather that the wicked turn from his way and live. Turn back, turn back from your evil ways! Why then will you die"—Ezekiel 33:11.

> Let the one who wishes take the water of life without cost—Revelation 22:17.

> Whoever believes in Him should not perish, but have eternal life—John 3:16.

God is doing all He possibly can right now to draw people to Himself. When we pray for the lost or witness to a person, we are not twisting God's arm into saving them; we are cooperating with Him in His effort to gather the harvest to Himself.

Workers Working Together

Jesus makes an interesting remark in the Gospel of John:

> "Do you not say, 'There are yet four months, and then comes the harvest'? Behold, I say to you, lift up your eyes, and look on the fields, that they are white for harvest. Already he who reaps is receiving wages, and is gathering fruit for life eternal; that he who sows and he who reaps may

rejoice together. For in this case the saying is true,
'One sows, and another reaps.' I sent you to reap
that for which you have not labored; others have
labored, and you have entered into their labor'—
John 4:35-38.

These verses show us that evangelism is work, which
is why Jesus asked us to pray for workers for the harvest.
While it is God's work, He has chosen not to do it all by
Himself and has called us to be co-laborers with Him. (See
1 Corinthians 3:9; 2 Corinthians 6:1; Mark 16:20.)

Regarding this work of evangelism, someone has said,
"Without God, man cannot. Without man, God will not."
So, the work of evangelism is a cooperative venture. We must
be sure we do our part in close cooperation with God, in
much the same way Jesus was intimately united with the
Father and did only what He saw the Father doing. (See John
5:19.)

Cooperation is important not only between ourselves and
God but also between us and our fellow workers. Unity, after
all, is to be the visual sign for the world to believe the
gospel. (See John 17:21-23.) According to Psalm 133:3, God
commands a blessing—'life forever'—when believers are in
unity with one another. The blessing of life forevermore
is for the lost, not Christians, since we already have that
blessing. That blessing, however, will only be bestowed
when we flow together in unity.

We see in Acts that when the believers in the early church
were of "one mind," the Lord added to their number daily
"those who were being saved" (Acts 2:44-47). Later, after
some internal disunity was taken care of, God blessed them
by multiplying the number of disciples in Jerusalem, and
a "great many of the priests were becoming obedient to the
faith" (Acts 6:7).

In evangelism, God measures our effectiveness both corporately and individually. We are not a collection of saved souls but a many-membered Body united to bring glory and honor to our Head. As "members one of another" (Romans 12:5), we should live and work accordingly.

Seeing this Bible picture of the Lord of the Harvest directing workers who are patiently waiting for His command has totally changed my concept of witnessing and evangelism. Now whenever I have the opportunity to witness to someone, I know I have been sent to that person by the Lord either to break up the ground, plant seed, water, or reap the harvest.

Before going out in evangelism, I now ask the Lord to lead me to those He has prepared so that I can do the required work and see the person brought closer to salvation. If I talk to someone and they receive Christ, then I try to follow up on them or arrange for another worker to do so. If the person doesn't receive, I ask the Lord of the Harvest to send along another worker to take up where I left off. In this way, God coordinates the efforts of His workers in all parts of the harvest field, responding to prayer and sending those who have made themselves available as His workers wherever He sees work that needs to be done.

Leading Of The Spirit

Mark, a twenty-three-year-old Californian, had gotten involved in drugs and found only emptiness, so he had turned to Zen Buddhism. After eight months of Zen discipling at a retreat center in the Sierra mountains, he abandoned the mystic route and hitchhiked south to warmer weather.

Near Santa Cruz, Mark was picked up by a Bible college student, John, who proceeded to share the gospel with him. Mark listened but was still heavily influenced by the teachings of eastern mysticism, especially reincarnation. When he informed John that it was taught in the Bible, John was ready with an answer. (See 1 Peter 3:15.) He spent the next two hours with Mark, talking, answering his questions, and showing him from the Bible that it teaches not reincarnation but resurrection. John broke up the ground of Mark's heart and planted the seeds of the gospel there. After dropping him off, he prayed that the Holy Spirit would convict him of sin and lead other workers to water what had been planted in Mark's heart.

One morning soon afterwards, as I prayed, I felt the Lord impressing on me that I should go witnessing downtown. By divine appointment, I came across Mark, handed him a tract, and began sharing with him about Jesus. After about fifteen minutes of conversation, we parted; but before he left I gave him the address and phone number of my church and invited him to come along sometime. I prayed that night, as I always do after having the opportunity to witness, that God would give increase to the work I had done that day and that more workers would be sent into the harvest field. (See 1 Corinthians 3:6; Luke 10:2.)

Walking along a beach several days later, Mark struck up a conversation with a Christian who was having a quiet time. After a brief introduction, Scott began to question Mark about his relationship to the Lord. Mark admitted that he didn't have a relationship with God but had been seriously thinking about it lately. Scott realized that Mark was not ready for harvesting quite yet and did not lead him in the sinner's prayer; instead, he gave Mark the address of his church (which was the same as mine) and invited him to attend.

A few weeks later Mark did come to church, heard the gospel again, and went forward to the altar to give his life to Christ. From there he moved into our community "The Land," and was discipled. Today he is a Bible teacher being trained for missionary service.

In this example, the workers the Lord used were sensitive to the needs of the particular person they were dealing with. John didn't have a self-righteous attitude about Mark's belief in reincarnation and patiently took the time to show him the truth. The other workers, also, were not "sickle happy" and ready to cut the first signs of growth but were sensitive to the Lord's timing and the needs He wanted them to address in Mark's life. The result of this patient sensitivity to the Spirit was the lasting salvation of Mark.

Spiritual Abortions

After preaching at an open-air meeting on Union Square in San Francisco, I was approached by a woman who introduced me to her non-Christian friend from Germany. She was interested in the message I had preached and asked me many questions about Christianity. I patiently answered them and discussed more about the gospel with her, all the while trying to sense her need. In the midst of our conversation, her friend interrupted with, "Don't worry about your doubts; just ask Christ into your heart. The feelings will follow."

That woman had made the same mistake many of us make when we imagine that the sinner's prayer is a cure-all for the woes of the unbeliever—if only they'll just accept Jesus, then everything will be okay! We must not forget, however, that it is essential for a person to believe *before* they are persuaded to receive. We must be patient with the non-believer and not hurry them into something they are not ready to receive wholeheartedly.

Paul told Timothy,

> The Lord's bondservant must not be quarrelsome, but be kind to all, able to teach, patient when wronged, with gentleness correcting those who are in opposition, if perhaps God may grant them repentance leading to the knowledge of the truth, and they may come to their senses and escape from the snare of the devil, having been held captive by him to do his will—2 Timothy 2:24-26.

This scripture shows us four agents involved in conversion: (1) *the Christian witness* (Romans 10:14); (2) *the non-Christian with a free will* (Romans 10:13); (3) *the truth of the gospel* (Romans 10:17); and, (4) *God* (John 6:44; Matthew 16:17).

The non-Christian is under the snare of the devil, so we must be aggressive with our work in the harvest field. But this sometimes involves patience, and we must wait while God deals with someone He is drawing to Himself. "Behold, the husbandman waiteth for the precious fruit of the earth, and hath long patience for it, until he receive the early and the latter rain" (James 5:7, *KJV*).

When dealing with people I am seeking to win to the Lord, I haven't always exercised patience. For example, shortly after becoming a Christian, I moved out of the house where I had been living, realizing that the atmosphere of sex, drugs, and rock and roll was not conducive to my spiritual growth.

I left that house with a burden to see my old surfer friends, and in particular my closest friend, Dave, won to the Lord.

Being such a young Christian, I was big on zeal and small on wisdom. I would drive over to my previous house to share the gospel but would inevitably end up feverishly pressing Dave to make a decision for Christ. Using fear, bribery, manipulation, and all the soul power I had, I thought it had worked as I drove Dave to the ocean to baptize him. On the way there I explained about the rapture, the mark of the beast, the common market, and the antichrist that would soon arise, hoping to reassure him about his decision. But, as we walked out into the ocean, Dave told me he wasn't sure he was ready to go through with it. I assured him he was and dunked him under the water in the name of the Father, Son, and Holy Spirit. I told him that since he had prayed the sinner's prayer, the feelings would soon follow.

It didn't take long for me to realize, though, that I hadn't really led Dave to the Lord. All I had actually done was get a sinner wet! I had manipulated Dave into saying a prayer that he didn't really mean in his heart. He didn't believe the gospel, he hadn't repented of his sins, and he surely didn't want to follow Jesus.

Proverbs 18:13 tells us, "He who gives an answer before he hears, it is folly and shame to him." Dave had answered before he had really heard because I was not patient enough to allow God to draw him to Himself. In fact, my interference actually slowed down the Lord's dealings with Dave to the point where I had to go back later and replant the seed in his heart—seed that would eventually bear fruit. Jesus promised that all those who reap *while the harvest is ripe* will gather "fruit for eternal life" (John 4:36). Several years later Dave did give his life to the Lord in a sincere and lasting way, and today he is still one of my close friends, as well as a growing disciple.

Careless Sinners And Seekers

In essence, the harvest field contains only two types of people. There are those whom Charles Finney categorizes as "careless sinners," content with the present state of their life and happy sitting in unbelief and spiritual darkness. Then there are "seekers," who are spiritually hungry and diligently searching for truth. These are the people who, if not challenged with the gospel, often end up in religious cults or other causes that offer to satisfy their hunger for truth. We need to be sure that we are challenging both categories of people with the gospel.

Jesus illustrated these two types of people in His parable about the man who found a treasure in a field and the parable of the pearl merchant. (See Matthew 13:44-46.) The pearl merchant could be described as a seeker, "seeking goodly pearls." The other man is like the careless sinner, who, after stumbling upon treasure hidden in a field, went and sold all he had to buy the field. Mark, mentioned earlier, could be categorized as a religious seeker. We must not lose hope for those who presently are not seeking at all.

Several years ago, Phil and Rebecca, a young couple who lived together, drove their pick-up truck down to Santa Cruz. There, Dawn, an old high-school friend of Rebecca's, had arranged for the three of them to get together. Dawn had recently become a Christian and was anxious to share her new faith with them. After several minutes of her witnessing, however, Phil told her in no uncertain terms that he didn't want to hear any more on the subject. Dawn was sensitive to this and for the next couple of weeks just prayed for them, befriended them, and spent time with them practicing light shining evangelism.

One day she took them to a local beach, where some young people happened to be playing slow motion football. Inquisitively, Phil walked over to ask what they were doing, and one of the players, a clean-cut eighteen-year-old college student, told him they were part of a summer outreach team and were using the football game as a tool to share the good news of Jesus Christ. He asked Phil if he had ever heard of the four spiritual laws. Phil admitted he hadn't, so they spent time discussing them together.

Their conversation was fairly broad, ranging from the four spiritual laws to modern events and the current world situation (remember interest doors?). As they parted company, the student gave Phil a copy of Hal Lindsey's best-selling book, *The Late Great Planet Earth*. Phil accepted it readily and took it home to read.

Dawn, meanwhile, was continuing her visits with them. One day she took them to an elderly Christian lady's home for apple pie and ice cream. Margaret, the elderly lady, told them how good it was to be saved and shared her testimony with them while serving the pie. She also invited them to "The Land," our community, for dinner that night. At that time I had the privilege of leading them both in a prayer to accept Jesus. Today they are strong Christians and involved in the ministry. These two fitted our second category of people: They were not seeking spiritual truth, yet through many different people's diligent witness, they were brought to salvation.

The Lord Of The Harvest

In Phil and Rebecca's testimony, we see the parable of the seed-planter illustrated. The ground of their heart was hard, but Dawn plowed it up and softened it with love, friendship, and intercession. The Lord of the Harvest then went on to use the student on the beach, the four spiritual laws tract, Hal Lindsey's book, the loving testimony of an elderly saint, and even a physical place, "The Land," as tools to draw Phil and Rebecca to Himself.

The above illustration raises an important question: Which one of us actually led them to Christ? As the one who led them in the sinner's prayer of commitment to Jesus, was I entitled to two notches on my Bible cover? Actually, the Bible tells us that it was the Father who led them to Jesus. (See John 6:65.) It is the Father who reveals to the unbeliever who Jesus is. (See Matthew 16:17.) And it is the Spirit who convicts of sin. (See John 16:8.)

If we would only realize that God is the soul-winner and we are only helping Him carry out His work, then we would see fewer Christians reveling in the glory that should be God's alone. We must be careful not to see our evangelistic activities as spiritual scoreboards keeping track of how many souls each person has won to the Lord.

We must never take the credit for the fruit of the harvest field. Every time we have the unspeakable privilege of helping someone come to the Lord, whether by plowing, sowing, watering, or reaping, we should fall on our face in praise and exclaim, "To *God* be the glory, great things *He* has done!" We must make sure that God gets every bit of the praise for the fruit of evangelism: "But he that glorieth, let him glory in the Lord" (2 Corinthians 10:17, *KJV*).

"The harvest is plentiful, but the laborers are few; therefore beseech the Lord of the harvest to send out laborers into His harvest'' (Luke 10:2; see also Matthew 9:37-38). We are called to be workers in God's harvest, which is more ripe today than it has ever been. From around the nations of the world, reports continue to come in about the unprecedented receptivity of people to the gospel.

From Jesus' teaching on evangelistic farming, we can deduce that there would be an even greater harvest gathered into the Kingdom of God if He had more workers to work with Him. Jesus' brokenhearted cry goes out today with more urgency than when He first uttered it two thousand years ago. Will you be a worker?

7

Decisions Or Disciples?

CHAPTER SEVEN

Decisions Or Disciples?

"Go therefore and make disciples of all the nations, baptizing them in the name of the Father and the Son and the Holy Spirit, teaching them to observe all that I commanded you; and lo, I am with you always, even to the end of the age"— Matthew 28:19-20.

After I first heard God's call to be involved in evangelism, I would sit back and pipe-dream about how He was going to use me to evangelize the world. With an inflated ego and selfish desires, I saw myself giving the altar call in a multi-thousand seat stadium, calling the throngs to come forward and accept Christ. I was God's man of faith and power for the hour: "Come to Christ, hundreds of you, from all over the stadium. Come forward—the buses will wait!"

Indeed, in my early days, that was my highest ideal for effective evangelism: If we could just get enough evangelists to hold enough large rallies, have enough television and radio exposure, and mass distribute huge quantities of literature, then surely we would see the world evangelized in just a short time. As my experience in evangelistic work and my knowledge of the Word of God grew, however, I realized that my early perspective on evangelism was both impractical and short-sighted. While some sorts of mass evangelism are needed and crucial to God's plan, they are neither the only nor the ultimate way of reaching the world.

Follow-Up—The Key To Lasting Fruit

In the New Testament, evangelism and discipleship are closely linked, but they are not synonymous. A report by the American Institute of Church Growth indicated that at a 1976 Billy Graham crusade only 15 percent of those converted actually ended up as active church members one year after the crusade. (*Time Magazine*, January 23, 1978). This statistic is not quoted as a criticism of Billy Graham or mass evangelism. We acknowledge that his ministry has changed countless thousands of lives. Indeed, we should be praising God that the cup is 15 percent full, not complaining that it is 85 percent empty.

But this statistic does highlight an inherent weakness in mass evangelism: The evangelist cannot personally disciple all of his converts. He does not have enough time to sit down and listen as each individual pours out their hurts and needs and then see them established in a local church. He doesn't have the time to be a Paul to a thousand young Timothys. His job as an evangelist is to proclaim the gospel and call unbelievers to repentance and faith. We need mass evangelism—and every other type of evangelism for that matter—so that we can use "all means" (1 Corinthians 9:22).

At the end of an evangelistic crusade, however, personal workers must take the time to do the discipling. I believe one of our great needs right now is for individual Christians who will help others come to faith in Christ and then lead them on to spiritual maturity. We disciples must also be disciple-makers.

Billy Graham himself is quoted as saying, "The most important phase in an evangelistic campaign is the follow-up." This is because the object of the Great Commission is not merely to make converts but rather to see these converts become mature disciples and faithful members of a local church. We can see from the way Jesus trained His disciples and the strategy Paul had for church planting that God is not satisfied with seeing souls merely converted to Him. He wants these converts to grow into spiritually mature disciples. Jesus commanded us to go and make *disciples*, not just decisions.

As a new Christian, I had no idea of the biblical relationship between evangelism and discipleship. I would go out on the streets witnessing, buttonhole someone, and press them to pray the sinner's prayer. When I achieved this objective, I would proudly go home and chalk up another soul for the Kingdom. But in light of the little lasting fruit I saw among my "converts," it wasn't long before I had to re-examine both my methods and theology of evangelism. In fact, many of the people I had "led to the Lord" still loved their sin, had no love for God, and had no desire to study the Bible or pray. Most of them didn't even want to talk to me again! I began to see a great weakness in my understanding of evangelism and its ensuing results.

Jesus said, "I chose you, and appointed you, that you should go and bear fruit, and that your fruit should remain" (John 15:16). This verse came as a revelation to me. Through it I learned that God was not impressed with how many decisions I had recorded. He was not interested in glowing statistics but lasting fruit in my evangelism. He wanted to see disciples made, not just decisions recorded. My shotgun type of soul-winning may have impressed my envious friends, but, as far as God was concerned, my results were not making the charts in heaven!

World Evangelism—One At A Time

Part of my responsibility as leader of a missionary sending base includes studying statistics on unreached people groups and seeking God for ways to reach them. To be honest, sometimes it's discouraging to realize that there are not just millions but billions of people on earth who have never heard the gospel. Then there are the millions who have heard it, rejected it, and need to hear it again.

Most of us have grown up in the "instant generation" and are accustomed to having almost anything we desire within just a few moments. From McDonald's hamburgers to power tools and word processors, we have learned that anything we want is within easy reach. Unfortunately, our "instant" mentality has crept into our view of evangelism. Those of us from the western world have a tendency to set unobtainable goals in our pursuit of souls. When these are not achieved, we are left feeling discouraged.

Once, in a prayer meeting, we were lifting up requests for fruit in individual evangelistic endeavors. With characteristic Western zeal, one of the girls in the meeting exclaimed, "I claim a million souls to Christ—this year!" I said a sheepish "amen" to this request and thought to myself, *Sister, if you've got the faith, then go for it!* She didn't win her million souls to the Lord, and I have yet to speak in a soccer stadium; but does that mean neither of us is successful in evangelism? Should we feel discouraged and ineffective? After all, what is successful evangelism?

If we had been Jesus, I think we would have been very discouraged as we saw the "multitudes . . . scattered abroad, as sheep having no shepherd" (Matthew 9:36, *KJV*). But Jesus was not discouraged. He had a plan—a deliberate strategy— He was going to implement during His three and a half years of ministry on earth. He knew that the most effective way to minister to the multitudes was through multiplication—multiplication of Himself in His disciples so that they in turn could minister to the throngs.

Throughout Scripture, we see Jesus calling His disciples aside to instruct them in His ways. This strategy at first seemed long and arduous, but the results of it would be long lasting. Jesus avoided the obvious temptation to try and reach the multitudes all at once, knowing that if He took the time to pour Himself into the twelve and disciple them, they, in turn, could go and disciple the multitudes.

In his book, *The Master Plan of Evangelism*, author Robert Coleman points out that in the course of Jesus' three and a half year ministry, He spent increasingly more time training the twelve and increasingly less time ministering to the multitudes. While not totally neglecting the masses, He was far more concerned with His long-range objective—making disciples of all nations—than He was with any shortcut that in the end would actually prolong reaching His goal. To quote Coleman:

> You cannot outwit the powers of darkness without strict adherence to Him who alone knows the strategy for victory. . . . Only the Master's plan will work. . . . This is a question that should be posed continually in relation to the evangelistic activities in the church. Are our efforts to keep things going fulfilling the Great Commission of Christ? Do we see an ever-expanding company of dedicated men reaching the world with the gospel as a result of our ministry? That we are busy in the church trying to work one program after another cannot be denied. But, are we accomplishing our objectives?[1]

The Timothy Principle

Paul's challenge to Timothy was to gather faithful disciples who could learn from him and in turn train other faithful disciples: "And the things which you have heard from me in the presence of many witnesses, these entrust to faithful men, who will be able to teach others also" (2 Timothy 2:2). The key word in this process is "faithful," not talented, rich, charismatic, or good-looking.

Proverbs 25:19 says, "Confidence in an unfaithful man in time of trouble is like a broken tooth, and a foot out of joint" (*KJV*). Having had both broken teeth and sprained ankles, I know for a fact that you can't put confidence in either. God wants faithful disciples who will stick to His strategy for victory (even in times of trouble), seek out other faithful disciples who want to grow, and pour themselves into them until *they* can disciple others. The Lord wants those who are willing to win, train, and send out others to do likewise for the cause of world evangelism.

How do we go about making a disciple? In Matthew chapter twenty-eight, Jesus gives us the answer: "Go therefore and make disciples of all the nations, baptizing them in the name of the Father and the Son and the Holy Spirit, teaching them all that I commanded you" (Matthew 28:19-20).

First we must *go* to the person, and then we must seek to lead them to faith in Christ and seal it with baptism. What follows is sometimes a long and painstaking process in which the new believer is taught to follow and obey Jesus in every area of their life. We must be prepared for this to take time and answer their questions, teach them the Scriptures, and help establish them in a local church. We must become the new disciple's friend and be willing to spend time just being with them. Jesus "appointed twelve, *that they might be with Him*" (Mark 3:14, *italics added*).

In disciple making, Jesus told us to teach them to obey all His commands, and that includes His last commandment—to go and make disciples. We must be disciple-making disciples!

An important advantage in the Timothy principle for the multiplication of disciples is that most Christians are not mass evangelists and would feel uncomfortable ministering to large crowds. They may not be able to believe God for hundreds to come forward at a crusade, but they can believe for one they can take and disciple. I challenge you to ask God today for a Timothy. Win him, train him, and send him back to the world to do for someone else what you have done for him.

Multiplication And Addition

A simple comparison of multiplication and addition reveals the wisdom of the Timothy principle. Imagine, for example, an evangelist winning one thousand people to Christ every day, working 365 days a year with no time off. In thirty years of ministry, he will have added over ten million people to the Kingdom of God.

Now imagine a Christian like you, who is capable of winning one person a year to Christ. You spend your year discipling this lone convert to the point where he can go and disciple another. He then spends his next year winning and discipling another. In the meantime, you are also discipling another, and so the process goes. If this were to go on unbroken, it would only take nineteen years to win ten million people to Christ—all because of your initial willingness and involvement. We can see that if the world is going to be evangelized, then we must use principles of multiplication, not just addition.

Several years ago I took a team of twenty-three Discipleship Training School students from *Youth With A Mission* to Fiji for a three-month outreach. During the first half of the outreach, we were involved in door-to-door evangelism, street witnessing, ministry in local churches, and a Thursday night new believers Bible study. On Saturdays we held an open-air meeting downtown, which was reaping good results.

Things were going well until the immigration department informed us our tourist visas would not permit us to continue our activities. They told us that we could do no more ministry whatsoever—not even sing a song in a church.

We were all very discouraged by this and began to seek the Lord for a new strategy. God soon showed us that we must obey the ruling of the immigration department and stop all ministry. So I challenged each student and staff member to ask God for two people they could win and disciple during the remainder of our time in Fiji. My thinking was that if we could leave behind forty-six transformed Fijians, then our outreach would have been fruitful.

Some of the team began following up on people they had led to the Lord during the first half of the outreach. Others discipled nominal Christians who had no grounding in their faith. Some went out as tourists and asked God to lead them to the right people. Still others began befriending the neighbors and reaching out to them. This was all accomplished without the ministry tools we were so used to—guitars, tracts, Bible studies, open-air meetings, and the like.

In evaluating the success of this outreach several months later, I was delighted to find that two churches we had worked with had baptized thirty new members who were now attending regularly and growing in their relationship with God. There were other new disciples in several other churches, and many nominal Christians had been strengthened in their faith. God's principles of evangelism do work; after all, He is the one who designed them and gave them to us in His Word.

The Timothy principle also spreads out the work load of evangelism. More people are able to be released to the work of evangelism, so the load is shared among a greater number of workers. There is also less chance of someone getting all the glory for the fruit produced.

Ephesians chapter four teaches on the five-fold ministry of the Holy Spirit. We find that apostles, prophets, evangelists, pastors, and teachers have all been given to the church for "the equipping of the saints for the work of service" (Ephesians 4:11-12). In other words, "professional" ministers aren't called to do the primary task of ministry but are to equip the saints, the average Christian, to undertake that task. *We need to see that we are all called to be God's ministers of reconciliation* and in so doing are His ambassadors and priests. (See 2 Corinthians 5:18-20; 1 Peter 2:5-9; and Revelation 5:10.) All of us must be involved in the work of discipling.

The Joy Of Discipleship

I will never forget the day the revelation hit me that God could actually use *me* to bring someone to Himself. I was in a worship meeting, and, looking across the aisle, I saw my friend Steve worshipping God with his hands raised.

Steve and I first met when I picked him up hitchhiking and gave him a ride home. I had known Steve as an unbeliever, and then I had the joy and privilege of seeing him come under conviction of sin and finally surrender his life to the Lord. As I reflected on it in church that day, I realized that God could use even me, an unworthy servant, as an instrument in His hands. I began to weep with joy and thanksgiving. Leading a person to Christ is one of the greatest feelings a person can ever have in this life.

I think the only greater thrill in life is seeing someone you have led to the Lord lead someone else to the Lord in turn. As the bumper-sticker says, "Happiness is Being a Grand-parent," and I can assure you that my greatest feelings of joy in the Christian life have come from seeing my spiritual children reproduce themselves. Imagine the joy it must have brought to Jesus as He looked down the corridors of time and prayed for His disciples and all those who would come to believe in Him because of their testimonies. (See John 17:20.)

Paul, too, must have been beside himself with joy when he learned his spiritual offspring, the Thessalonians, had

> . . . become an example to all the believers in Macedonia and in Achaia. For the word of the Lord has sounded forth from you, not only in Macedonia and Achaia, but also in every place your faith toward God has gone forth, so that we have no need to say anything—1 Thessalonians 1:7-8.

John told Gaius that he could have no greater joy than to hear that his spiritual children were walking in the truth. (See 3 John 4.)

Realizing the link between evangelism and discipleship, and that people needed a place where they could grow into mature Christians, I began praying for a house similar to the Shekinah House in Santa Cruz, where I had been discipled. God, however, provided not one but five houses on a piece of property right in the heart of town. We named it "The Land," and a handful of us moved in.

As a young leader at "The Land," I went through my share of frustrations and changes. We faced every kind of trial imaginable—discouragement, set-backs, disappointment, financial problems, lives being threatened, and rip-offs; but through everything, including my spiritual immaturity, God was able to use "The Land" to bring people to Himself and see them discipled.

What a joy it is for me to recount some of the lives that were changed for the glory of God during this period. I remember Danny, who had just arrived in town from New York when I met him. He had been in five different mental institutions by the time he was twenty-one, and, while in New York, he had attempted suicide three times. Danny was gloriously saved and mentally healed, and today he is a missionary in Japan.

Then there is Kevin, an ex-Moonie, who moved in with us at "The Land" after his conversion. Within several years he was a missionary in the Philippines, where he is an elder and leader in *Youth With a Mission*.

Scott, who was saved and discipled by us, is now a missionary in Japan, while Larry, who used to grow marijuana in his backyard, became a missionary to Nepal after he was converted and discipled at "The Land."

Frank was converted at a Jack-in-the-Box restaurant and was discipled by us. He is now leading a *Youth With A Mission* School of Evangelism that trains and sends missionaries to Asia.

I mention these people not to take any credit for myself but to illustrate the necessity of discipleship. As we take the time to train and ground new believers in the faith, they in turn can be released to go and make other disciples.

A Look At Wesley's Methods

John Wesley believed that the world was his parish. He organized his converts into small groups where "the beginnings of faith in a man's heart could be incubated into saving faith in the warm Christian atmosphere of the society, rather than in the chill of the world."[2] Understanding implicitly the Biblical connection between evangelism and discipleship, Wesley put as much emphasis on discipleship as he did on soul-winning. The result of this was one of the most powerful evangelistic and missionary movements in church history. It is said that he "would refuse to preach in any place where he could not follow it up by organized societies with adequate leadership."[3]

Wesley's ministry is best summed up in these few short words: "He was out to make disciples—disciples who would renew the whole church."[4]

Baby Care

One of the most dangerous things I have observed in the Body of Christ is the insensitive way we treat new Christians. Whenever a baby is born, he or she gets all the attention, as mommy, daddy, grandparents and friends all gather round to goo-goo and gaa-gaa, tickle, and enjoy this new life that has come into the world. In a similar way, this care and attention should also be extended to baby Christians, who have been born-again.

Just as a baby explores his new environment, looking and crawling around and getting into everything within reach, so spiritual babies need the liberty to do the same. Suddenly, they are in a new environment—the Biblical Christian culture—and are expected to be at Bible studies, prayer meetings, praise times, and the like. This may take them by surprise. We must be sensitive and realize that a baby Christian doesn't grow into a spiritual giant overnight. It takes time, and we must allow them the liberty of that time.

Those of us who are older in our relationship with the Lord especially need to watch that we don't require more obedience from a new believer than God does. A mother, after all, will expect a lot less from her two-week-old infant than from her eight-year-old son. In our zeal to preach repentance, sometimes we add on to God's commands and expect more faith from a baby Christian than they have the capacity for.

Statistics have shown that younger Christians are often the most effective soul-winners, and there are several reasons for this. They still have a zeal and excitement about the Lord. Since they haven't become so immersed in the Christian culture that they are alienated from the world, they still have unsaved friends. But one of the main reasons for their effectiveness is that they can understand and relate to both unbelievers and new Christians, since they themselves are often still spiritual toddlers.

When I was first converted out of the drug culture, I earnestly believed my dog, Joshua, was going to go to heaven. I wanted to move into the Shekinah House for discipling, but I refused unless Joshua could come with me. I desperately needed discipling, but my dog was a high priority in my "baby" mind. Fortunately, the brothers leading the ministry loved me and were sensitive to my needs. They gave me some breathing room and allowed Joshua to move in with me. Looking back now, I praise God for their understanding and tolerance.

Another friend of mine, Kerry, was selling ounce-bags (lids) of marijuana when he got saved. After his conversion, he proceeded to add gospel of John booklets as a bonus to the lids he was selling! Now, that was a dumb thing to do! It was a baby thing to do, but someone was loving and kind with Kerry and showed him a more excellent way. Soon he stopped selling dope altogether.

Gary was also newly saved out of the drug culture. The Holy Spirit began to deal with him about selling drugs, and one day Gary gathered up all his marijuana and took it to the beach. There he made an altar and offered the drugs as a burnt offering to the Lord! From there, Gary went on to become a strong Christian and effective soul-winner, but he started out as a baby.

Be nice to baby—you'll be glad you did!

8

Thy Kingdom Come

(The Missions Mandate)

CHAPTER EIGHT

Thy Kingdom Come

(The Missions Mandate)

In response to His disciples' question on how to pray, Jesus gave us what has come to be known as the Lord's Prayer. In this prayer, the very first petition we are instructed to place before the Father is that His Kingdom will come and His will be done on earth as it is already being done in heaven: "Pray, then, in this way: 'Our Father who art in heaven, hallowed be Thy name. Thy kingdom come. Thy will be done, on earth as it is in heaven' " (Matthew 6:9-10).

If it is God's will for His Kingdom to come on earth, then what on earth is the Kingdom of God? The answer to this question is crucial if we are to understand Christian missions properly.

From the beginning, God has desired that mankind rule over all His creation. When He had finished His original handiwork in Adam and Eve, God blessed them and told them,

> "Be fruitful and multiply, and fill the earth, and subdue it; and rule over the fish of the sea and over the birds of the sky, and over every living thing that moves on the earth"— Genesis 1:28. (See also Psalm 8:4-6; Hebrews 2:6-8.)

Through their fall, however, Adam and Eve forfeited the right to rule on earth as God had intended. But God was not to be side-tracked from His original plan by their rebellion—He had purposed in His heart that His Kingdom *would* come.

God then called a Babylonian named Abram and declared His intent to bless him and make him a blessing to all the peoples of the earth. (See Genesis 12:1-3.) Through Abram, God was going to raise up a nation that would represent His rule (or Kingdom) to all the nations. (See Exodus 19:5-6; Deuteronomy 30:1; Numbers 14:20; Psalms 67,96,98; Isaiah 49:5-6; 66:18-19; Zechariah 9:9-10.)

On several occasions God repeated this promise to Abram and then confirmed it with an oath, swearing by Himself. (See Genesis 22:15-18; Hebrews 6:13-19.) Isaac and Jacob also received the promise that their offspring would be a blessing to all peoples of the earth. (See Genesis 26:4; 28:14.)

For the most part, Israel failed in its God-given mission, so God had to establish the Levitical priesthood. The nation chosen to be a kingdom of priests now *needed* priests (the Levites) themselves because of their failure to obey God's plan. Eventually, God's own Son would have to declare to the Jews, "The kingdom of God will be taken away from you, and be given to a nation producing the fruit of it" (Matthew 21:43). The nation Jesus Christ has now chosen is the Church (1 Peter 2:9), and the "fruit of it" is the obedience of Jew and Gentile to the King of the Kingdom. (See Matthew 3:8; Luke 3:8-9.)

The Gospel Of The Kingdom

The word "kingdom" in both the Old and New Testaments refers to the right to rule or the authority exercised by a king.

Psalm 103:19 declares, "His Kingdom rules over all." But beginning with the fall, Satan has led captive—out from under God's authority—a host of rebels. When Jesus returns, however, He will establish once and for all God's Kingdom in all its fullness. Every knee will bow in submission to Him—whether the knee-benders like it or not! (See Philippians 2:11.) In the meantime, our job is to preach the gospel of the Kingdom and give people the opportunity to bow their knees willingly—before it is too late. (See Matthew 24:14.) We are to occupy (keep busy at His work) until He comes. (See Luke 19:13.)

The Great Commission to reach all nations was not just some afterthought Jesus had when He established the New Covenant. It has been God's plan from the beginning. He has always wanted to rule all the peoples of the earth lovingly and righteously. Paul tells us the gospel of grace and the gospel of the Kingdom are one and the same: "And the Scripture, foreseeing that God would justify the Gentiles by faith, preached the gospel beforehand to Abraham, saying, 'All the nations shall be blessed in you'" (Galatians 3:8).

The command to be a blessing to all peoples—and so extend God's Kingdom—given to Adam, then Abraham, Isaac, and Jacob is the very backbone of the Bible. (See Acts 3:25; 13:47; Romans 1:5; 16:26; and Revelation 5:9; 7:9.)

Blessing, Fruitfulness, And Multiplication

We find that as God gave His "Kingdom mandate" to Abraham, Isaac, and Jacob, He also gave the three promises of *blessing, fruitfulness,* and *multiplication* along with it. (See Genesis 12:3; 17:6-20; 18:18; 22:17; 26:4; 26:24; 28:3.) Today, as then, God wants to bless His people.

These blessings are not meant to be ends in themselves but the means for us to be fruitful and multiply! God, who was blessed in Himself, created man to share that great blessing so that those of us who are "of faith are blessed with Abraham" (Galatians 3:9). And just as Abraham became a channel of blessing to all peoples of earth, we must be, too.

Throughout history, God's people have had a tendency to hoard His blessings to themselves instead of passing them on. Jesus gave specific instructions for the early disciples to carry the gospel to "Jerusalem, and in all Judea and Samaria, and even to the remotest part of the earth" (Acts 1:8). Despite this mandate, they stayed on in Jerusalem— even after fierce persecution had driven all other Christians out of the city to those places God had intended for them to go. (See Acts 8:1-4.)

Apart from occasional short missionary trips, the original apostles stayed on in Jerusalem despite Jesus' instruction for them to go to the remotest parts of the earth.[1] Perhaps this is why the Holy Spirit chose to focus most of the book of Acts on Paul, the apostle who obeyed God's command to be "a light for the Gentiles" (Acts 13:46-47).

Following Paul's example, Christians for the next two and a half centuries went everywhere and preached the gospel. Eventually they saw the whole Roman Empire surrender to and embrace Christianity. Shortly after this, however, the church began to lose its missionary zeal and doctrinal purity. For the next thousand years the Great Commission was largely forgotten as the church entered the Dark Ages.

During the Reformation under Luther, Calvin, and Zwingli, the church still was not fully committed to its obligation of reaching the ends of the earth. This was due in part to Luther's belief that the second coming of Christ was so imminent that there wasn't time for world evangelism and that the Great Commission was binding only on the original apostles. For the most part, the doctrine of *justification by faith* remained locked up in Europe. We are given no evidence that the Reformers actively sought to allow the gospel to be fruitful and multiply cross-culturally.

The flame of world evangelism did not get rekindled until 1727, when Count Nicolas Zinzendorf established the Moravian missionary movement. Motivated by the slogan, "May the Lamb that was slain receive the just reward of His suffering," missionaries landed on all six continents in just twenty years. Within one hundred and fifty years, over two thousand Moravian missionaries, most of them young, had been sent overseas. Indeed, it was Moravian missionaries who led John Wesley to faith in Christ. They also greatly influenced William Carey, who was to become known as the "father of modern missions."

Carey carried the torch lit by the Moravians, and in 1792 published his classic work, *An Enquiry into the Obligation of Christians to use Means for the Conversion of the Heathen*. In 1793, Carey himself sailed for India, but his publication fueled the fire of missions. Soon there was much interest in evangelism and missions in England, Scotland, Holland, and America. Where there had been little concern for the unreached groups in the vast regions of Asia, Africa, India, and Latin America, now Christians were anxious to see the gospel shared among these people.

During the last century, Hudson Taylor's pioneer work into China released another wave of missionaries to new frontiers. Over six thousand missionaries were served by Taylor's China Inland Mission, and his vision to reach into the interior of unreached nations became the impetus for scores of other mission organizations. Since that time, many others have followed the principles of Carey and Taylor and gone out to the ends of the earth to preach the gospel.

Because the foundations of world evangelism have been well laid, we can optimistically look from our vantage point in the 1980's and see all that is being done worldwide to further the gospel of God's Kingdom. While there are still areas of the world that lie in darkness, the church is flourishing in many others.

For example, in Brazil about three thousand new churches are established each year. In Africa and Asia one thousand new churches open their doors every Sunday. The church is growing so fast in Africa that by the year 2000 nearly 50 percent of the population south of the Sahara will be Christian. In many parts of Latin America it grows three times faster than the population. The numbers of protestants there has soared from 50,000 in 1900 to well over twenty million in 1980.

Asia is also experiencing unprecedented church growth. In South Korea, where there were virtually no Christians at all one hundred years ago, today close to 30 percent of the population acknowledges Jesus Christ as Lord. The same is true of Indonesia, Singapore, the Philippines, and parts of India, where tremendous growth has also taken place in the last several years. In all, approximately 78,000 new Christians are added to the worldwide Body of Christ daily.[2]

It is interesting to note, however, that Europe has replaced Africa as the "dark continent." It is the only region on earth where Christianity is actually *decreasing* in numbers, as secularization and liberal theology have joined hands to push back the gospel. The Muslim world, with its eight hundred million inhabitants (mostly in the Middle-East, North Africa, India, and Indonesia), is the most resistant region to the gospel. This is due in part to a lack of workers. Although this region constitutes nearly 25 percent of the world's population, only one percent of the North American missionary force is working there.

Along with the Muslim world, the other areas of greatest need for missionaries are: the Chinese (one billion), Hindus (600 million), and Buddhists (250 million). The challenge before the church of the 1980's and 90's is still great, but it is a challenge that is surpassed by the opportunity we have to spread the gospel to the ends of the earth. The opportunity is before each of us, and the promises of God are with us—Jesus said GO!

Get Involved Now!

There is no time to waste. Every day that we remain indifferent to our responsibility to obey the Great Commission is a day lost to the cause of Christ. God wants us to see the world as He sees it, having a global perspective of His eternal purposes in Christ.

I first began to see God's perspective on the world several years ago on a trip to Disneyland with my family. We were on a ride called, "It's a Small, Small World," where little boats go through tunnels into imaginary countries. In these countries are dolls of all the different nationalities on earth. All the dolls sing with glee, as if they didn't have any cares, "It's a small world after all." There they were—dolls from Holland, China, Arabia, America, Spain, Russia, and Africa, all holding hands and smiling happily in their native costumes. Suddenly I began to weep. By the time we had reached the end of the ride I could hardly see through the tears in my eyes.

When we came out into the light again, my wife looked at me, shocked, and my son Daniel asked me what was wrong. I tried to express to them what I was feeling: "It's not a small world. It's not a happy world. It's a wicked, dirty, sinful world, and for the most part it's being run by the devil, while people are singing their way to hell!'' The people, waiting to go on the ride looked at me like I had gone crazy, and Daniel wasn't exactly sure what to make of his daddy, either.

I suddenly saw on that ride that the storybook image of the small world is exactly what Satan wants us to see so he can keep us indifferent to the millions who perish without Christ. Don't get me wrong—I'm not saying Disneyland is of the devil, but neither does it portray reality as God sees it.

The fact is that a harvest is ripe in a field with painfully too few workers: ''Lift up your eyes, and look on the fields, that they are white for harvest'' (John 4:35). We must become an army of World-Christians who are not content just to be ''normal.'' We are not normal, we are *ecclesia*— ''the called out ones''—called out from the darkness of this world into the light so we can rescue those still perishing in darkness without Christ.

The normal Christian life is to be the radical Christian life. It should be as different from the lifestyle of this world as light is from darkness. As we learned from Abraham's life, God has blessed us so that we in turn will be a blessing to the nations of the earth.

Burden, Vision, And Work

The book of Nehemiah gives us insight into three ways we can become involved with God in His global cause. Nehemiah hears of the awful plight of his brethren in Jerusalem who have survived the captivity. The city wall is broken down (symbolic of lack of protection from enemy), the gates are burned with fire (symbolic of burned-out evangelism), and the people are in distress. After hearing this news, Nehemiah immediately sets himself to pray, fast, and seek God's face over the situation.

1. *Developing The Burden.* Nehemiah didn't have to seek God for a burden—he already had one, so his fasting and praying was a natural reaction to hearing the news that God's work was in trouble. He was *already* close to God's heart, so when God was burdened he was burdened. Indeed, holiness has been defined as hating what God hates and loving what He loves. As a branch abides in the vine, it begins to take on the characteristics of the vine, one of which is a love of righteousness and a hatred of evil.

By "burden" I mean having a concern for the things God is concerned for and not a heavy down-on-everything attitude that leads to legalism. After all, Jesus said His burden was light; but it was nonetheless a burden. (See Matthew 11:30.) Do you think God is concerned about the three thousand language groups who still do not have Scriptures in their own language or the 16,750 distinct ethnic people groups who have no Christian witness among them? What about the nearly one billion starving and malnourished people in the world and the millions of babies killed every year by abortion—does God care about them?

Yes, I believe God is vitally concerned about these situations. He wants us to share this concern (or burden) with Him so that we, in turn, will do something about it. There are two ways we can develop this burden for the world: First, we can pray for and intercede on behalf of those who are in darkness. As we draw close to God in this way, He is able to impart to us His heart for a situation.

The second way to develop a burden is simply to get involved. Often people who are actively involved in reaching out to the lost are unaware of the weight of the burden they carry since seeing needs and meeting them moves them in both prayer and action.

2. *Catch The Vision.* Someone has said, "A vision without a burden makes imagery; a burden without a vision makes drudgery; but a burden with a vision makes a missionary." Soon after Nehemiah had prayed and fasted about the situation in Jerusalem, God turned his burden into a vision. He began to see the city wall rebuilt, the gates re-hung, and the people in safety. In much the same way, we must allow God to expand our vision for a situation so that we will be motivated to action.

God will never give us a burden for a situation unless He also intends to give the positive side of it—a vision to see the situation changed. Moved with a burden of compassion at facing a workerless but ripe harvest field, Jesus implanted a vision in His disciples to see themselves as workers for the harvest. (See Matthew 9:36-38.)

All major endeavors for God start with a burden that later becomes a vision. For instance, William Booth's burden for the down-and-outs of London was turned into the vision of the *Salvation Army*. The *Heart of Africa Mission* was started by C. T. Studd after he received a burden for the tribes of darkest Africa. In the same way, *Teen Challenge* was born out of David Wilkerson's burden for inner-city youth, and Loren Cunningham's burden to see young people used in missions resulted in the birth of *Youth With A Mission*.

What is your vision? Do you believe God can use you in an active way in His global task of reaching the nations? Maybe you think you're not qualified enough. You're probably right! But then, neither was Jeremiah: "I do not know how to speak, because I am a youth" (Jeremiah 1:6).

Nor was Gideon's army qualified when just three hundred men went to battle the Midianites, who were "innumerable" (Judges 6:5; 7:6). As Gideon's army came close to the point where it would be cut to its final size, God instructed him to take the remaining ten thousand men down to the water for their final test. Those who had their own needs as top priority—the ones bowing down on their knees to drink, their eyes fixed only on the water—were sent home. Those who lapped the water out of their hands while their eyes scanned the horizon for danger were the ones God was interested in using to demonstrate His power through. In His wisdom, God chose only three hundred men to fight the hoards of Midianites, but they were three hundred men of faith and vision.

To catch the vision for world evangelism and the multiplication of God's Kingdom that can come through us, we can learn a lesson from Gideon and his army. They weren't fearful at all but trusted God and fixed their eyes on Him and His ability to defeat the enemy through them. We need to examine ourselves to see where our heart really is in relation to God's work. But we must also avoid the pit-fall of "onion peeling" introspection, where the more we peel, the more it stinks and the worse we cry! (See 2 Corinthians 13:5.) Once we have examined ourselves, then we must fix our eyes on Jesus, where, like Gideon's army, our needs will be met.

3. *Doing The Work.* The book of Nehemiah ends happily with the work on the city wall being completed. This was a direct result of Nehemiah's obedience to the burden and vision God had given him. After God has given us a heart for and perspective on a particular situation, He also expects us to be available to Him so He can work through us and fulfill His desire. This, after all, is the meaning of seeking the Kingdom first.

Ultimately, the work of evangelism can only be accomplished when each of us does our own individual part in building up the Body and cooperating with others who are also doing their part: "The whole body, being fitted and held together by that which every joint supplies, according to the proper working of each individual part, causes the growth of the body" (Ephesians 4:16).

God has chosen to use many different parts all working together to fulfill His purposes for world missions. Listed below are some practical ways that you can become involved in the work of missions and take the gospel of Jesus to the nations of the world:

1. *Short-Term Missions.* My concept of a missionary had always been of a square who, because he couldn't make it in normal life, would bury himself in the jungles among the pygmies of Africa. Or, sometimes I thought they were someone like the bigot Abner Hale in Michener's "Hawaii," who sought to destroy the native culture.

My first missionary experience came on a *Youth With A Mission* short-term outreach to Fiji in the South Pacific. Here I worked alongside a group of people who were just like me. They weren't squares, weirdos, or bigots. They were normal people committed to taking the gospel cross-culturally, in a sensitive way, to the people of Fiji. Once I had tasted world missions in this setting, I was hooked for life.

Perhaps a short-term outreach or unholy land tour is what you need to get a realistic picture of what missions is all about and what a missionary really does all day. This type of experience can be valuable whether or not you feel God is calling you to the mission field. Organizations such as *Youth With A Mission, Operation Mobilization (OM),* and others have various short-term programs and special outreaches worldwide in which you can be involved. These programs all provide exciting, hands-on missionary involvement and may well whet your appetite for more!

Some groups, *YWAM, OM, Last Days Ministries*, and *Horizon International*, for example, offer short-term discipleship training opportunities that lead directly to missions involvement in just a few months. Perhaps you could consider this after high school, before you get settled into college or a career.

2. *Mercy Ministries.* Many groups offer both long and short-term involvement in everything from food distribution, medical work, and nutritional services to building and providing shelter for people. War, natural disasters, and famine in recent years have created a vast need for this sort of specialized work among the twenty million plus refugees scattered across the face of the globe. Many of these people have been stripped of everything except life itself. Jesus said that if we serve the least of His brethren, then we are in turn actually serving Him. (See Matthew 25:40.)

3. *Bible Translation.* Of the 7010 distinct living languages in the world today, there is no translation of the Bible in over 3000 of them. Wycliffe Bible Translators and other groups provide practical linguistic training and help for those who desire to see God's Word translated and published among every "tribe and tongue and people and nation" (Revelation 5:9). Dedicated long-term workers are needed in this area to assist at all stages of the translation process.

4. *The Smaller Half Of The World.* Today, over 50 percent of the world's population is under eighteen years of age. Children require a specialized strategy of evangelism that is suited to their particular needs. Many evangelical missions have formed specialized branches of their organization to minister to this needy and open area of child evangelism. Perhaps God is calling you to this ministry.

5. *Support Workers.* David told his people that those who stayed home to look after the baggage would get the same rewards as those who were on the frontlines of the battle. (See 1 Samuel 30:24.) Many missionary organizations require several support workers for every missionary on the front lines who is doing the direct work of evangelism. Administrators, secretaries, public relations people, accountants, kitchen workers, mechanics, construction workers, and maintenance people are all needed to keep the machinery of missions moving toward its objective. No matter what talents you have, God can use them effectively in missions.

6. *Support Givers.* Missionaries are mostly supported in their endeavors by people like you and me who give voluntary contributions toward their work. In regard to this, one of the questions I am often asked is, ''Why aren't missionaries today self-supported like Paul?'' There are several answers to this question. First, in order to preserve jobs for their own people, many countries do not issue work permits to foreigners. Second, the less concerned a missionary has to be with making money to pay his living costs, the more time he or she can spend involved in the work of the gospel. After all, that is the only reason he is in the country. Third, Paul wasn't always self-supported and gladly received financial aid from various churches. (See Philippians 4:14-18.)

We need to make it our practice to give generously and regularly to missions. Perhaps the best way to do this is through giving directly to the worker in the field. Giving this way is advantageous because it lets you know exactly where your dollar is going. At the same time, you will feel personally involved in their ministry. This should be a two-way thing, however, and the person being supported needs to communicate regularly what he is doing to those supporting him.

Each year Americans give one billion dollars to missions. While this sounds like a wonderful contribution, we need to consider that we spend nearly that amount yearly on chewing gum and seven times as much on pet food! Perhaps this will stir us to dig a little deeper in our pockets the next time we hear of a missionary who has a need.

7. *Church Planting.* Jesus Christ commanded us to go and make disciples of all nations. In light of this command, we need to be pioneering churches that will nurture and establish disciples in God's Word among the sixteen thousand people groups who have no permanent Christian witness. Pioneer church planting is perhaps the most barren area of missions work today. Many young people are desperately needed to lay down their lives by going to an unreached area, learn the language and culture, evangelize, and eventually plant a church there. They also need to be committed to staying until local leaders are strong enough to assume the responsibility of running the church and caring for the spiritual needs of the area.

Establishing and multiplying churches, I believe, is the battlefield where world evangelism will be won or lost. We need an army of committed people in every area of the harvest field who are following Paul's methods—establishing churches that will multiply themselves, training up national leaders, and moving on to establish another church elsewhere. (See 2 Corinthians 10:16.)

Ultimately, church planting is the bottom line in world missions. After someone has been won to Christ, they must have a structure into which they can fit and feel comfortable as they grow and reproduce themselves. All missionary work is a means to an end: making disciples—disciples who need nurturing and training.

Short-term evangelistic teams and traveling evangelists should keep this in mind and endeavor to work closely with existing, solid evangelical churches in the area where they are working. If there are no churches that can mold strong disciples out of new converts, then one needs to be established. Too many spiritual abortions have taken place because well-meaning evangelists have lost sight of their long-term objectives. We must constantly monitor our results to see if we are achieving what we set out to do.

I was converted during what is now known as the "Jesus Movement." One of the characteristics I noticed about this movement was an unquenchable zeal for outreach by converted ex-dopers and hippies. There was a strong emphasis on both personal and mass evangelism in the form of street-witnessing, street-preaching, door-to-door evangelism, and literature distribution, as well as gospel concerts, marches, and rallies. As the movement developed on into the 1970's, there was a swing toward discipleship with an emphasis on teaching, training, and equipping the believers. We began hearing much about Christian community, church unity, and relationships within the Body. At that time the cassette tape ministry began to boom as pastors were busy about the job of feeding their sheep.

In the 1980's, I've noticed a swing back toward evangelism, but with a more mature emphasis. Most church leaders now agree that evangelism without follow-up and discipleship without an evangelistic thrust are faulty. Groups that have no vision of multiplying themselves are in danger of becoming mere Christian country clubs and catching the disease someone has termed "koinonitus"— an overdose of fellowship! Nature shows us that inbreeding within the same family will produce deformity, and the same is true in the spiritual realm.

I believe God has been laying the groundwork for a mighty end-time thrust of the gospel that will reach to every corner of our world. We need the evangelistic fervor of the

1960's coupled with the call to commitment heard in the 1970's so that we will have mature, calculated strategies for reaching the world. God is raising up an army that in these last days will overcome the devil by "the blood of the Lamb and because of the word of their testimony" and by not loving "their life even to death" (Revelation 12:11).

God wants modern day William Careys and Hudson Taylors who will pioneer frontier regions of the world for Him. He wants disciples who aren't just engaged in theological controversy and debate—who aren't arguing about the timing of the second coming but are out busily proclaiming the good news of what Jesus did at His first coming. He wants an army that won't be asking, "How much does it cost?" but rather, "Where do I pay?" They won't want to know how much sin they can get away with and still be saved. Instead they will ask, "How much can I do to further the Kingdom?"

Our heavenly Father wants people who are consumed with love for Him, whose desires are one with His, and who won't be content until the earth is "filled with the knowledge of the glory of the Lord, as the waters cover the sea" (Habakkuk 2:14).

I challenge you to ask God seriously if He wants you to go. Perhaps He wants you to be a modern day pioneer who will change the eternal destiny of a nation that presently sits in darkness. Be willing, obedient, and trusting; He always has your highest good in mind. If He tells you to go, then go. He will take care of the details. If He does not tell you to go, then pray. Pray for specific areas of the world and the missionaries who are on the front lines. Maybe He wants you to support financially one of those whom He has called to go.

Go For It, Brethren!

Jesus said, "I have come to cast fire upon the earth; and how I wish it were already kindled!" (Luke 12:49). Evangelistic zeal is like a fire and needs to be fed and stoked continually to keep it burning hot. Human nature tends toward coldness and indifference to spiritual things, especially gospel work when it becomes uncomfortable. Re-read this book and study the Scripture passages referred to or quoted so that your fires of zeal will continually be stoked by the consuming desire to see the Great Commission completed.

Seek out and get to know other brothers and sisters who are single-minded about missions and who can be examples for you of the lifestyle of evangelism. Read biographies of people God has greatly used in evangelism. Talk about evangelism, revival, and missions with your Christian friends so that you encourage one another to love and good works. (See Hebrews 10:24.) Share with your friends those books and tapes that have moved you to a deeper commitment to God and His purposes. Above all, however, begin to witness where you are, remembering that you learn to witness *by witnessing*. It may be hard at first, but allow God the time to start a fire in you—a fire that will spread to those around.

Lastly, and by far most importantly, get close to Jesus. As we draw close to Him, He begins to rub off on us—His desires become our desires and His plans our plans. Spend time with Him. Spend days in secret fasting and prayer alone with Him. If you diligently abide in Him, He has *promised* you will bring forth fruit that will remain. (See John 15:16.) When the Lord returns, may He find each one of us busy *bringin' 'em back alive*!

NOTES

Introduction

1. Green, Michael. *Evangelism in the Early Church* (Grand Rapids, MI: Eerdman's, 1970), p. 278.
2. Wagner, C. Peter, editor. *Church Growth—State of the Art* (Wheaton, Ill: Tyndale, 1986), p. 53.

Chapter 1

1. Winter, Ralph, editor. *Perspectives on the World Christian Movement: A Reader* (Pasadena, CA: William Carey Library Publishers 1981), p. 271.
2. Green, Michael. *Evangelism in the Early Church* (Grand Rapids, MI: Eerdman's, 1970), p. 274.
3. Lawson, J. Gilchrist. *Deeper Experiences of Famous Christians* (Anderson, IN: Warner Press, 1970), p. 247.

Chapter 2

1. "Heritage Factor": Term coined by Jim Peterson in *Evangelism as a Lifestyle*, (Colorado Springs: Navpress, 1980), p. 46.

Chapter 3

1. Wagner, C. Peter. *On the Crest of the Wave* (Venture, CA: Regal, 1983), p. 141.
2. Miller, R. Edward. *Thy God Reigneth* (East Point, GA: Argentine Bible Assemblies of God, 1964), p. 35-39.
3. Quoted in, Braun, Jon. *Whatever Happened to Hell* (Nashville: Thomas Nelson, 1979), p. 86. (He was citing an article in *Christianity Today,* August 6, 1976, by Edward Fudge called "Putting Hell in it's Place."
4. Bonhoeffer, Dietrich. *The Cost of Discipleship* (New York: MacMillan, 1967), pp. 47-48.

Chapter 6

1. Yeakley, Flavil. *Why Churches Grow* (Colorado: Christian Communications, 1979), p. 65 in *State of the Art*, edited by C. Peter Wagner (Wheaton: Tyndale, 1986), p. 60.

Chapter 7

1. Coleman, Robert E. *The Master Plan of Evangelism* (Old Tappan: Revell, 1979), p. 11.
2. Gould, J. Glenn. *The Hurt of Man* (Kansas City: Beacon Hill Press, 1971), p. 65.
3. Diamond, Sydney C. *The Psychology of the Methodist Revival* (London: Oxford Press, 1926), p. 112.
4. Snyder, Howard A. *The Radical Wesley* (Downers Grove: Intervarsity Press, 1980).

Chapter 8

1. Richardson, Don. *Eternity in Their Hearts* (Ventura: Regal, 1981), p. 156.
2. Barret, David. *World Christian Encyclopedia* (New York: Oxford University Press, 1982).

APPENDIX A
Recommended Reading

Lifestyle Evangelism

1. Peterson, Jim. *Evangelism as a Lifestyle* (Colorado Springs, CO: Navpress, 1981).
2. Peterson, Jim. *Evangelism For Our Generation* (Colorado Springs, CO: Navpress, 1985). (These books by Jim Peterson are two of the finest books on incorporating evangelism into your daily life.)
3. Pippert, Rebecca. *Out of the Salt Shaker* (Downer's Grove, IL: Intervarsity Press, 1979). (An excellent book, from a woman's perspective, on the necessity of being "human" when sharing our faith. Provides a thorough examination of Jesus' methods of communicating the gospel.)

Street Evangelism

1. Blessitt, Arthur. *Arthur A Pilgrim* (Hollywood, CA: Blessitt Publishing, 1985).
2. Blessitt, Arthur. *Arthur Blessitt's Street University* (Hollywood, CA: Blessitt Publishing, 1977). (These two books by Arthur Blessitt are a guaranteed turn-on to evangelism. They are by a man who, probably more than any other, has challenged the church to a lifestyle of evangelism.)

3. Gainsbrugh, Johnathan. *Take Him to the Streets* (Shreveport, LA: Huntington House, 1985). (Perhaps the most practical book available on street evangelism. It contains hundreds of helpful tips on street evangelism from a man who is dedicated to the task of sharing the gospel.)

4. Gibson, Noel. *The Fisherman's Basket* (Lawson, Austrailia: Freedom in Christ Ministries, 1984). (This is the most complete book available on open-air ministry. A must for any would-be street preacher.)

Inspiration For Evangelism

1. Finney, Charles G. *Revival Lectures* (Old Tappan, NJ: Revell, 1979). (A strong challenge to evangelism, revival, and fervent prayer by America's foremost revivalist.)

2. Spurgeon, Charles. *The Soul Winner* (Grand Rapids, MI: Eerdman's, 1963). (Inspirational lectures on soul-winning by the "Prince of Preachers.")

Discipleship Evangelism

1. Coleman, Robert. *The Master Plan of Evangelism* (Old Tappan, NJ: Revell, 1979). (A biblical examination of Jesus' strategy for world evangelism. Excellent reading.)

2. Eims, Leroy. *The Lost Art of Disciple Making* (Colorado Springs, CO: Navpress, 1978). (Practical help and teaching on individual discipling.)

Missions

1. Cunningham, Loren. *Is That Really You God?* (Old Tappan, NJ: Revell, 1984). (The exciting story of *Youth With A Mission*, with practical help on guidance and inspiration for missions.)

2. Richardson, Don. *Eternity In Their Hearts* (Ventura: Regal, 1981). (An excellent, inspiring book revealing God's strategies in bringing the world to Christ.)

3. Wagner, C. Peter. *On the Crest of the Wave* (Ventura, CA: Regal, 1983). (A concise, in-depth look at how the machinery of missions actually works.)

4. Winter, Ralph and Hawthorne, Steve, editors. *Perspectives on the World Christian Movement* (Pasadena, CA: William Carey Library Publishers, 1981). (An 800 page, 81 chapter examination of the biblical, historical, cultural, and strategic perspectives of world missions.)

APPENDIX B

A SAMPLE TRACT

Presented below is a sample of a tract I have written and used in my evangelism. It is provided here to show the type of tract you could put together for your evangelism; or, perhaps you may like to copy this one and use it. It is also provided as a model presentation of the gospel, one that you could adapt and use in your conversations with unbelievers.

THE FACTS OF LIFE

Fact No. 1

God loves us and wants to give us eternal life:

> For God so loved the world that He gave His only begotten Son, that whosoever would believe on Him should not perish, but have everlasting life—John 3:16.

God loves each one of us personally. We are the highest of all His creation, being made in the image of God. (See Genesis 1:27.) Each one of us is unique and special to Him. Our Heavenly Father desires with all His heart that we would choose to live in His family forever.

Fact No. 2

We are separated from God because of our sins:

> All have sinned and come short of the glory of God—Romans 3:23.

Each one of us has sinned, or broken God's law, which He has given us for our good. (See 1 John 3:4; Deuteronomy 6:24.) Sin displeases God and hurts us and our fellowman. When we choose to live in sin, we are separating ourselves from God.

Fact No. 3

The penalty for our sins is death:

> Death passed upon all men because we have sinned—Romans 5:12.

> The wages of sin is death—Romans 6:23.

When we break man's laws we must pay a penalty for our actions. In much the same way God, in His justice, has laid down a just penalty for our sins—spiritual death and eternal separation from Him and His life.

Fact No. 4

Jesus Christ died and rose again to save us from our sins and the penalty of sin:

> . . . Jesus, He will save His people from their sins— Matthew 1:21.

Through Jesus' death on the cross, and resurrection, He promised to break the power that sin has over our lives if we would trust and obey Him (Romans 6). He also took the penalty for our sins upon Himself (Hebrews 2:9) and opened the door for us to be forgiven.

WHAT MUST I DO?
1. Repent
Make the choice to turn from all known sin. (See Acts 3:19.)

2. Believe

Trust in Jesus Christ, God's Son and His death on the cross for your sins. (See 1 Corinthians 15:3.)

3. Follow

Determine to follow Jesus as your Lord and Master, whatever the cost. (See John 12:26.)

My good friend: The purpose of this tract is to present to you as clearly as we can, the gospel of Jesus Christ. Becoming a disciple of Jesus is not joining a religion or a philosophy but beginning a relationship with God as our Father. This is the relationship He created us to have—to be His children. Jesus has shown us His love by giving His life for us. Will you give your life to Him?

STEPS TO CHRISTIAN GROWTH

1. Prayer

Talk to the Lord as your friend. (See Matthew 6:6.)

2. Bible Study

God's Word is food for your soul.

3. Fellowship

Find a Bible-believing and Bible-teaching church or fellowship and attend regularly. (See Hebrews 10:25.)

4. Witness

Share your faith with others. (See Luke 24:46-48.)

For information about:

* *Bringin' 'Em Back Alive* seminars in local churches
* *Bringin' 'Em Back Alive* audio tape series
* Short-term missions opportunities
* *Frontier Peoples Project* (church planting among unreached peoples)

Write:

> *Danny Lehmann*
> *Youth With A Mission*
> *P.O. Box 61700*
> *Honolulu, Hawaii 96839*
> *USA*

An 8-hour video teaching series on *Bringin' 'Em Back Alive* is available from:

> *P.A.C.U. Communications*
> *75-5851 Kuakini Highway*
> *Kailua-Kona, Hawaii 96740*